5-15-84   8.95

THE ALPS

Text by
PIERRE LEPROHON

Translated by
DAVID MACRAE

MINERVA

Designed and Produced by
Editions Minerva SA, Genève

Printed in Italy

INTRODUCTION

They stretch across the heart of Europe, from Nice to Vienna, covering half a dozen countries with a fantastic chaos of rock and ice, trapping the turbulent waters of a host of rivers to form spectacular lakes.

They are the watershed of Western Europe. Moreover they separate two climatic zones—north and south. They could even be said to be the frontier between two worlds, the Anglo-Saxon and the Latin.

The remark is also true when we consider Europe in the other direction: in the west the influence of the Atlantic reaches far inland, while the east has a continental climate, the warm air off the Hungarian plains.

The Alps... Voltaire called them "those haughty mountains which weigh down upon hell, and split the heavens". They were long thought of as a frightful place, into which travelers ventured only at their peril, the realm of death and silence.

But there is life hidden among the ice and snow. Hardy shoots of vegetation cling to the rocky crags at great altitude; grass waves in the wind at the rim of huge abysses. Then we come to the enormous upland pastures, strewn with wild flowers such as gentian, and the great coniferous forests, with their endless interplay of light and shade.

The Alps are, with the wealth of their diversity, the quintessential mountain range, forever asso-ciated with mountain climbing, to which they have contributed, *inter alia,* a synonym—*alpinism.*

These awesome mountains are also sublime sources of passions which vary quite as much as the rocky peaks themselves. For the mountain climber they signify action: the view from the top is worth less than the feeling of accomplishment. Staying there for another hour adds nothing to the experience. High mountains tend to over-whelm thought, leaving it fettered and earth-bound.

At this frontier between the mineral and living worlds—one in which the mineral element lives—we see the truth in Rousseau's remark: "High in the mountains, meditation takes on a grandiose and sublime character... a curious tranquil desire wholly lacking in sensuality and pungency".

This "tranquil desire" is attuned to the gentle pace of the mountain walker. The kind of thrills which inspire the skier racing down the icy slopes are very different indeed.

Whatever the country, the region or the alti-tude, the Alps offer a greater wealth of delights than one could hope to find in any other mountain range.

The Mont Blanc massif reflected in the waters of Chamonix, the capital of mountain climbing in France. Below, the famous *aiguilles* on the massif.

THE MONT BLANC MASSIF

The 'rooftop of Europe' is situated at a point where three countries meet. It is a prodigious cap of ice and snow which weighs down on the massif from which the 'cathedrals of the earth', as Ruskin called them, rear their peaks towards heaven: the Aiguilles du Midi and du Géant, La Verte and Les Drus.

At 15,770 ft. the highest peak in Europe, Mont Blanc sends its rivers of ice, with their bluish abysses, reaching out into the valleys: the Glacier des Bossons, the Mer de Glace, the Talèfre and Argentière glaciers, and the Vallée Blanche.

The valley of the Arve forms a deep gash in the heart of the massif, between the Aiguilles Rouges and the dome of Mont Blanc, of which the Grandes-Jorasses are an extension. The steep slopes, with their dense cover of pine forest, occasionally open out to form upland pasturages —natural 'balconies' from which one can at a glance take in the entire range of glaciers.

Down in the valley there are a number of resorts—which were just villages only a few years ago—and which now provide the delights of the outdoor life all year long to throngs of city-dwellers: Le Fayet-Saint-Gervais, Les Houches, Planpraz and Argentière. In the middle of the valley lies Chamonix—Chamouni—the Mecca of mountain-climbers, at the foot of the slopes.

In the 12th century this was the site of a Benedictine priory which eventually formed the nucleus of a village. St. Francis of Sales resided there in 1606. In the 18th century, two young Englishmen—one of them a student in Geneva—discovered the marvels of this strange landscape and became its fervent promoters. They attracted their compatriots with such success that the first inn opened at Chamouni was named the Hôtel de Londres by its owner, Jean-Pierre Tairraz, many of whose descendants are still living in the area.

Another Chamoniard, called Bourrit, devoted his life to his love for the mountains. It was he who led the first tourists, including some eminent people such as Goethe, who went there in 1779, to the Mer de Glace, near Montenvers. Bourrit never completed the ascent of Mont Blanc.

In August 1786 Jacques Balmat and Dr. Paccard were the first to reach the top—an exploit to be repeated the following year by de Saussure.

Then in the 19th century came the conquests of the most hair-raising peaks. Alpine mountain-climbing was born.

One of the *aiguilles* above Chamonix; a sweeping view of the resort; Place Balmat, with the statue of the guide after whom it is named—the first man to scale the summit, in 1786; right, the Mer de Glace (8.5 miles). A view of the massif; the entrance to the tunnel which links France to Italy directly beneath Mont Blanc. Following pages: reflections of the Mont Blanc massif in the tranquil waters of the Lac des Gaillands.

Nowadays the highest cable car in the world, that of the Aiguille du Midi, at 12,470 ft., and several others carry one effortlessly to the high points on the mountain range.

The Mont-Blanc massif, however, is special in that it caters not only to intrepid climbers, but is also a source of endless walking trails for lovers of solitude and silence. There are a number of shelters *(refuges)* along the way: at the Col d'Anterne, from which it is possible to reach the Col du Brévent, Le Couvercle at 8,830 ft., Leschaux at the foot of the Grandes Jorasses, and the Refuge Vallot, built in 1938 on a rocky spur in the midst of the icefields, for the benefit of climbers aiming at the peak.

The hiking circuit around Mont Blanc takes several days for a walker in good condition, via the Col du Bonhomme, the Col de la Seigne and Courmayeur, in Italy, which is now linked to Chamonix by a tunnel eight miles long, beneath a mass of rock over 8,000 ft. thick!

THE LAKE RIVIERA
AND THE CHABLAIS

Shaped like an arch, as are the Alps themselves, Lake Léman, or Lake Geneva, has such a mild climate and a charming landscape that it qualifies as a genuine lakeside Riviera. From Saint-Gingolph to Yvoire, on the south shore, a succession of promenades, villas, casinos and gardens which have preserved the true flavor of the past gaze out over the changing waters of this inland sea.

The two main resort towns, Evian-les-Bains and Thonon-les-Bains, rather than rivaling each other, are in fact mutually complementary. At Evian, with its Belle Epoque casino and its yachting harbors, a splendid divided avenue runs along the lakeside. Vineyards, orchards and groves of chestnut trees stretch away inland.

Thonon, built in terrace-style above the lake,

the former capital of the Chablais, provides delightful glimpses of the lake at the end of every block. Rives, down at the lake, is an old fishing village which has some fine historical remains: houses with outside staircases, a medieval tower and a 13th-century castle.

Both towns have their modern achievements too: the Palais des Congrès and the Centre Nautique at Evian, and the Maison des Arts et Loisirs, and the thermal spa at Thonon. Actually both of them have a reputation for curative waters: in the case of Thonon, those of the Versoie, for kidney trouble and arthritis; and the waters of Evian which are used for hypertension and also arthritis; there is also, of course, the famous mineral water, annual output of which runs into some 850 million bottles!

The fashion for health-giving waters began, however, with a nearby resort, Amphion-les-Bains. It was particularly popular during the Second Empire, but its high social standing was wrested from it by Evian, which continued to become more and more chic as the decades went by. Swimming, yachting and boat-trips are among the pleasures the lake has to offer nowadays. In summer there is a regular service all the way around Lake Léman, or along the the shore as far as Swiss territory.

The lakeside Riviera also has its hinterland—the Chablais which sweeps up from the lush green landscape of Bas-Chablais to the Gavot region, with the Pic de Mémise, a belvedere looking out over the lake, and Haut-Chablais high in the Alps.

Three main roads lead up the valleys from Evian and Thonon: one goes in the direction of La Chapelle d'Abondance, another towards Mor-

zine, a leading winter sport and summer hiking resort. Further up, at 5,900 ft., is the recently founded resort of Avoriaz, with its strange architecture near the ski slopes, the ice rink and the heated pool. With its radio-dispatched sleighs and discotheques, its night clubs and festival of fantastic films, Avoriaz has spared no effort to woo its clientèle!

The Alps on the French side of Lake Léman: the harbors of Évian-les-Bains and Thonon. Above: view of the picturesque village of Yvoirex. Following: modern buildings at Avoriaz.

WONDERFUL SAVOY

Between Geneva and Grenoble, between the comb of Savoy and the Rhone Valley, the three principal cities of Savoy—Annecy, Aix-les-Bains and Chambéry—are linked by an expressway and a network of secondary roads.

Each one has a lake, in a grandiose mountain setting: Le Semonz is reflected in the waters of the lake at Annecy, Aix-les-Bains has the Lac du Bourget, at the foot of Mount Revard, while Chambéry is situated not far from Lake Aiguebelette. These cities, at the threshold of the towering massifs of Beaufortin, Tarentaise and Vanoise, are both the past and the future of Savoy.

Beyond the Salève (4,526 ft.) which separates it from Switzerland, Annecy, which was settled in prehistoric times, later became a Gallo-Roman city and developed, from the 12th century onwards around its castle, of which the Tour de la Reine is today the oldest remaining part. Other dwellings were erected in later centuries, under the protection of the Tour Perrière.

At the foot of the rocky spur on which it stands —and which offers a fine view of the lake—the town was gradually built up and looked more or less like the old town in Annecy today. Arcaded streets, old houses along the quays, reflecting in the waters of the Thiou or the canals, old town houses and churches: the cathedral of Saint-Pierre (16th century), the church of Saint-Maurice, of the Dominicans, the church of Saint-François, the former bishop's palace (18th century) and the 12th-century Palais de l'Isle, once a prison—these are the monuments and places one should see.

Annecy is best known, however, for its lake, which is probably the finest in the region of the Alps. Beyond the public garden and the Champ-de-Mars a promenade runs along the shore. The Pont des Amours crosses the Vassé canal, where there is a multitude of small craft. Ile des Cygnes is a short distance offshore, while the slopes of Mont-Veyrier lie on the other side of these tranquil waters.

The village and the lake have their own special charm in each of the seasons, from springtime blossom to the rich foliage of autumn and the snows of winter. The pleasures are different, too: boating and swimming on the lake, trips into the mountains and around the town, where one is reminded of the memory of some of the famous people who have lived there.

Saint Francis of Sales—a local boy, since he was born at Thones—grew very fond of Annecy; he is buried in the basilica of the Monastery of the Visitation, near the tomb of Saint Jeanne de Chantal, an ancestor of Madame de Sévigné who founded the order. Moreover, while still an adolescent, Jean-Jacques Rousseau met Madame de Warrens and fell desperately in love with her.

Annecy is a charming prelude to the Alps—a place with a lake which lends itself uniquely well to boat trips. It stretches for about nine miles between moderate mountain slopes, from Annecy to Bout-du-Lac. It takes two hours to complete the boat tour around the lake, during which time

Three views of the Lac d'Annecy, one of the finest lakes in the Alps. Left, the medieval streets and the canals of Annecy.

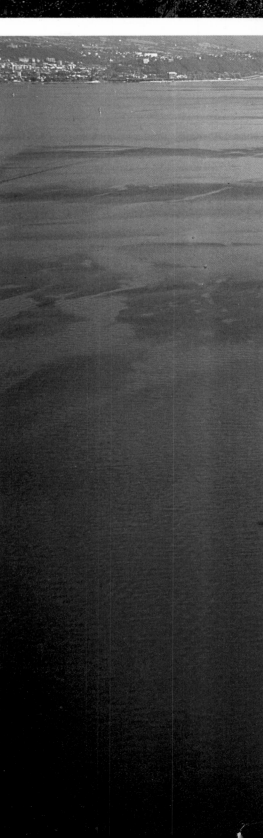

one sees the most attractive local sights. Veyrier-du-Lac has a cable car which goes up to Mont-Veyrier (4,265 ft). Menton has a château which stands in almost a military posture on the site of the fortress where Saint Bernard, the founder of the hospice, was born. Talloires and Duingt, two charming villages which one should visit, face each other across the narrowest point of the lake.

The Lac du Bourget, which is quite different in appearance, stretches from the Dent du Chat and La Chambotte. Some distance along the lake, and accessible from by both water and road, is Hautecombe Abbey, founded in 1139 and much restored over the ages. This handsome yet forbidding structure, which stands at the edge of the lake, is the pantheon of the House of Savoy. It contains the tombs of some forty princes and princesses: Humbert III, who had four wives, and Beatrice, who had four daughters, all of whom became queens—one of France, and the others of England, Germany and the two Sicilies.

The church, which was renovated in the 19th century, is sumptuously decorated with low reliefs and statues—of which there are more than 300, including a *Pieta* of Carrara marble and the effigy of Queen Marie-Christine by Albertoni.

The Lac du Bourget reminds us of Lamartine and his ill-fated love for Madame Charles, whom he immortalized in his poem *The lake:* "Oh time, suspend your flight, and you, kindly hours, suspend your flow!"

By the late 19th century Aix-les-Bains was already a renowned resort. In actual fact it had been popular since Roman times, though it was not until the 18th century that the first facility for treatment with warm natural spring water was established. The Thermes Nationaux we see today date from the end of the 19th century. Visitors can see the installations, some Roman remains and the cave from which the sulfurous water flows.

Moreover, Aix-les-Bains is a pleasant town to stay in for a while, being surrounded by mountains which serve as belvederes: the Chambotte, Dent du Chat, and Revard, a high wooded plateau from which a splendid forest road leads to Chambéry, with various stretches of corniche.

Chambéry, the third facet of the triptych, was the capital city the States of Savoy for several centuries. Its former splendor lives on in the castle which was once occupied by the princes. From the square there is a view of the old town, the Tour des Archives and the Sainte-Chapelle.

Annecy has his saint, Aix its poet and Chambéry its philosopher: Jean-Jacques Rousseau's memory is still present at Les Charmettes, the property of Madame Warrens, which was a "place of happiness and innocence" for the young student about the year 1740.

The landscape around Aix-les-Bains and, at Chambéry, the castle of the dukes of Savoy. Right, a view of the Lac du Bourget and the Benedictine abbey of Hautecombe.

FAUCIGNY AND BEAUFORTIN

Between the regions of Annecy and the Mont-Blanc massif, Faucigny and Beaufortin are two intermediate zones. The first of them consists of the parallel valleys of the Giffre and the Arve. Beyond the Risse Gorges, at the confluence of the river, the Giffre pushes its way through the tortuous Cirque du Fer à Cheval (Horseshoe Gulch), which consists of several miles of towering rock faces betwen 1,500 and over 2,000 ft. high. During the spring runoff, water comes cascading down from all directions. A path climbs up to the source of the Giffre, whose waters are derived from hanging glaciers.

Samoëns, at the heart of the limestone Faucigny, is a favorite place from which to go hiking and has an alpine garden which is due to the initiative of Mme Cognacq-Jay. A road leads north to the winter resorts of Les Gets and Morzine, in the Chablais.

The Arve Valley stretches from Bonneville, formerly capital of Faucigny, to Sallanches, via Mont-Saxonnex, which stands like a terrace over the valley, and Cluses. The Sallanches basin is the antechamber to the Mont-Blanc massif and offers climbers some splendid challenges along the Aravis range, the Rochers des Fiz and the Col d'Anterne. The most resort in these parts is certainly Mégève, with its vast ski runs, its excellent hotels and sporting facilities and its location, which has also made it a noted resort for natural therapy. The upper Arve valley, together with Le Fayet-Saint-Gervais and Les Houches already belongs to the Mont-Blanc massif.

Beaufortin, to the south, is a region of forests and upland pastures, the nature of which has been greatly changed by the Roselend dam.

Above: waterfall and pastoral landscape in the Tarentaise. The shore a small lake in Beaufort-tin. Facing, view of Les Arcs. Right-hand page, views of Megève and La Clusaz.

14

THE TARENTAISE

The Tarentaise consists essentially of the middle section of the Isère Valley, between Albertville, an old feudal city whose medieval remains look down over the new city which has been built on the right bank, and the Col du Petit-Saint-Bernard, which leads to the Val d'Aoste, in Italy.

Like that of the Romanche, this middle Isère Valley has fallen a prey to modern industry. It is not until we reach Bourg-Saint-Maurice, at the intersection of severals valleys, that we find a small alpine town in which honey and cheese for once prevail over steels and alloys!

Every summer the Fête des Edelweiss brings back to life, for one day, the pretty Tarentaise women's costumes, and the *frontière,* a three-pointed black velvet bonnet which is considered as the symbol of Savoy.

To the south the groups of villages known as Les Arcs form a ski resort whose chalets stretch out from 5,250 to 5,905 ft.

The main local peaks are La Grande Rochette, La Plagne and Mont-Pourri 12,395 ft.) and Pei-sey-Nancroix, which are served by modern facilities which seem to get more numerous with each passing year.

In the valley, Aime provides a link to La Plagne. Downstream, Moutiers, an old episcopal city which was once capital of the Tarentaise, has now become industrialized. However, it still has its Musée de l'Académie de la Vallée de l'Isère, housed in the former bishop's palace, and also the cathedral of Saint-Pierre, which was restored in the 19th century though some 12th-century parts still survive.

From Bourg-Saint-Maurice the road climbs to the Col du Petit-Saint-Bernard, at 7,178 ft., in the midst of the alpine pastures and boulder-strewn slopes. Beyond lies the Val d'Aoste, with a view of the Italian slopes of Mont-Blanc.

THE VANOISE AND THE MAURIENNE

La Vanoise is particularly well known nowadays for its National Park, the first in France, which was established in 1963. It covers 132,500 acres, with 362,500 acres of meadow-parklands—almost one third of the total area of the *département* of Savoie! The highest point is La Grande-Casse (12,640 ft.). Besides scenic beauty, however, this remarkable area is famous for its fauna and flora. In the past twenty years the wildlife populations have been restored to previous levels. It is now estimated that more than 2,500 chamois roam through this protected park, together with large numbers of ibex, marmots and ermine.

The flora is remarkably abundant, and includes ancolia and valerian, two survivors from the quaternary period. Another interesting species is the tiny arctic willow, which grows no higher than a few inches. There are numerous trails which lead across the park from the surrounding resorts, such as Val d'Isère, in the north, Pralognan in the west, Bonneval-sur-Arc, in the east and Termigon in the south. One excellent walk is a two-day venture, from Pralognan to Termigon, with stop-overs at the Félix-Faure and Entre-Deux-Eaux shelters. There is also a most enjoyable walk along the upper reaches of the Arc valley, via Bessans and Bonneval, as far as the Col d'Iseran (9,060 ft.).

For mountain-climbers, the Dôme de Chasseforêt, the Dent Parrachée and the Grande-Casse are ascents of more than 9,000 ft., though they can sometimes be difficult as the rock tends to be brittle. Hikers, on the other hand, have about three hundred miles of marked trails to lead them to new and exciting places.

Winter sports fans are well catered for by the new resorts of Les Ménuires and Méribel. However, these are no match for places like Courchevel, truly a metropolis of winter sports to the west

of the massif, and Tignes and Val d'Isère to the east.

Hydroelectric power—the 'clean' source of energy—has blackened the landscape! In lower Maurienne as well as in the middle valleys of the Romanche and the Isère, dams now supply power to large numbers of factories.

Lanslebourg-Mont-Cenis is the point of departure for the road to the Col du Mont-Cenis, at 6,830 ft., which is one of the main transit points between France and Italy. An observation platform has been built overlooking the lake formed by the dam.

The Mont-Cenis route has been known for centuries. Even as late as the 19th century, however, it was nothing more than a path which travelers descending the pass used to shun, preferring the kind assistance of the monks of the hospice who used to seat them on their sleighs and quickly sweep down the snow-covered slopes.

La Dent-Parrachée, on the other side of the valley, towers over the scene. Beyond it the frontier range drops abruptly on the Italian side.

Downstream from Lanslebourg, in the valley, Arvieux, Modane, Saint-Jean-de-Maurienne and Saint-Michel-de-Maurienne are fairly ordinary towns. Saint-Jean-de-Maurienne, a former capital city with a bishopric, has some historical reminders: a Romanesque cathedral, renovated in the Gothic style during the 15th century, and a cloister of the same period.

The name of the region, Maurienne, comes from *mau riau*, (or *mauvais ruisseau;* Eng. 'bad stream') on account of the disastrous floods of which the river is capable. Nowadays that same 'stream' is keeping the area busy and prosperous!

The Lac du Mont-Cenis, in Haute-Maurienne. The Col du Galibier. Modane, a frontier town. The Lac de Tignes. Right, views of the Massif de la Vanoise and the resort town of Courchevel.

GRENOBLE, THE METROPOLIS OF ALPINE SPORTS

A capital city—of the Dauphiné—in the heart of the French Alps; an old city whose name derives from *Gratianapolis,* for Emperor Gratian, and which has now become a metropolis expanding into all spheres, from industry to art, and culture to sport. Grenoble is a boldly designed modern town situated around the old quarters on the banks of the Isère, at the foot of the Fort de la Bastille, the local belvedere.

Amateur historians of all calibers will find the old town most rewarding. The church of Saint-André, with its stout square tower (13th century) and the mausoleum of Bayard, the Law Courts, formerly the Palace of the Dauphiné Parliament, with their Gothic architecture and Renaissance decoration, the picturesque Grande-Rue and Place Sainte-Claire, with the birthplace of Stendhal, the church of Saint-Laurent, in the district of the same name, whose origins can be traced back to the Allobroges, and lively Place Grenette —all combine to make this visit really attractive.

The museums are also worthwhile: the Musée Dauphinois for archeology and history, the Musée d'Histoire Naturelle, near the Jardin des Plantes, and the Musée des Beaux-Arts, one of the best fine arts museums in the French provinces.

The town has stretched out beyond this center area along broad avenues and through districts, such as Villeneuve, which have been described as experimental. The university city and the Olympic village built for the 1968 Winter Games, provide novel solutions to the problems of a steadily growing city.

But Grenoble is also, and perhaps primarily, the crossroads of Alpine touring. Beautifully situated between the massifs of the Grande-Chartreuse, Vercors and Belledonne, it leads to all the major resorts in the Dauphiné.

Le Moucherotte and Chamrousse, which are closer by, are fine vantage points from which to survey the valley and the mountains. As one might imagine, most of the young people of Grenoble are avid winter sports enthusiasts; in their immediate vicinity they find superb downhill and cross-country skiing at Chamrousse, Col de

Porte and the Col d'Autrans.

Chamrousse is specially equipped for handling huge classes of schoolchildren learning how to ski. As a resort it owes its reputation, and indeed its fine facilities, to the 1968 Olympic Winter Games. It offers something for everyone, from beginner to daredevil.

In summer it is a good place from which to go hiking up towards the Seiglières and the Belledonne peaks. Just to the south is the beginning of the Route Napoléon, so named because it was built on the route followed by the emperor on his return from the island of Elba, in March 1815. A statue has been built at Laffrey, in the Pré de la Rencontre, where the royalist troops who had been sent to halt his advance decided to join forces with him instead.

Left, the Oratoire du Chazelet and a general view of Grenoble. Below, a road in the vicinity of Allevard and the valley of the Grésivaudan, at the foot of the Belledonne massif.

THE CHARTREUSE MASSIF AND THE GRESIVAUDAN

Northeast of Grenoble, the Isère has carved out a huge valley between the Chartreuse massif and the Belledonne range. Chapareillan, some distance from what was once the frontier of Savoy, marks the northern limit of the area known as the Grésivaudan—or Graisivaudan. The busy life of the valley, particularly involving the production of hydro-electric power, is in sharp contrast with the solitude of the forests which cover the slopes of this vast corridor. This was the home of Bayard —the 16th-century "knight with neither fear nor reproach", whose memory lingers on in a surviving part of the ancestral castle.

Even in those days there were numerous monks in the monastery which had been founded late in the 11th-century by Saint Bruno and his companions. Anxious to find a way to withdraw from the world, they had been led to the "desert" by the bishop of Grenoble and the order—which took the name of the place—soon developed, on the basis of a rule which was never amended. The earliest buildings were buried by avalanches or destroyed by fire; those which we see there today date from the late 17th century.

The Chartreuse massif stretches from the outskirts of Grenoble to the Col du Grenier, along a succession of peaks, of which the most striking of which are the Charmant-Som (6,125 ft.), the Dent de Crolles and Chamechaude. Further back, the gorges of Guiers-Mort were, during the 16th century, the main means of access to the Chartreuse estate.

On the east side of the Chartreuse massif, the Route des Petites-Roches runs for about thirty miles in the shadow of the rocky faces of the massif, providing fine views of the Belledonne range and the Sept-Laux massif, on the other side of the Isère. Saint-Hilaire-du-Touvet, half-way along, is a climatic resort which may be reached

from the valley by the steepest cog-railway in Europe, with inclines of between 65% and 80%!

On the other side of the valley an equally picturesque road leads to Allevard, passing through the old villages of Laval and Theys which still retain their original character. Allevard has sulfurous waters and is situated in the center of a network of roads which make for some excellent trips, either on foot or by car, in the direction of Collet d'Allevard (4,755 ft.), a winter sports center with a ski chairlift which goes to the Grand-Collet (6,300 ft.), towards the Vallée des Huiles (a corruption of *aiguilles*, "needles") and the Chartreuse of Saint-Hugon.

Allevard also leads to the Sept-Laux massif (Laux = Lacs) along the high Bréda Valley. As little as thirty or forty years ago, this was an area of out-of-the-way hamlets and summer migrations of livestock; the dazzling lakes, at more than 6,000 ft. above sea level—Noir, Cotepen, Jeplan, La Sagne, etc.—are sometimes partially frozen even in midsummer.

A winter sports complex has been established at the resorts of Prapoutel and Le Pleynet. When completed, it is expected to stretch above Fond-de-France, which was once thought to mark the "end of the road" on account of its location. It is perhaps a pity that this very beautiful, scenic area was not declared a protected area before its development could start.

The monastery of La Grande Chartreuse, the buildings of which date back to the 17th-century. Left, the village of Allavard, and, right, the waterfall.

THE VERCORS

The name of this region has come to be identified with the French Resistance—and a symbol of a refusal to submit to foreign oppression.

Between the Drac and the Isère, the Vercors massif stands locked in by steep rock faces which would seem to want to prevent all access to it. It is covered the Vercors and Lente forests and deeply gashed by gorges such as the Grands-Goulets and Bourne.

In 1943 this difficult terrain seemed ideally suited as a center for the training of underground fighters and for actions designed to harass the occupying German forces. On 15 June 1944 a first offensive was launched, and Saint-Nizier was burnt to the ground. A month later there was fierce fighting around La Mure, La-Chapelle-en-Vercors and Vassieux. Nazi airborne troops dropped into the area and the enemy did their utmost to take this natural bastion. On 23 June Colonel Huet was obliged to give the order to disperse.

The guerrilla warfare was going to continue, but losses had been heavy: many civilians had

been massacred and their houses destroyed. There is a monument at Vassieux to the Martyrs of Vercors.

Peace now reigns at the scene of such carnage. In 1970 a national regional park was set up to protect nature and promote rural life. The flora of the massif is particularly striking. Forests stretch between upland pastures where cattle migrations still take place.

The Vercors is also a land of cave and potholes. Being a limestone massif which has been steadily and profoundly eroded it has provided potholers with an unending stream of discoveries. Berger cave, one of the deepest in the world, reaches a depth of 3,755 ft. Bournillon grotto, Malaterre gulf, and the Sassenage "vat" (cuve) are the principal cavities in the region, together with Luire grotto, where the severely wounded members of the Resistance had been assembled. They were discovered and massacred by the enemy.

Summer is the preferred season for potholers, but winter provides skiers with exceptional opportunities for cross-country skiing. Villard-de-Lans, capital of this white wonderland, is situated on the Lans plateau, which enjoys exceptionally long hours of sunshine in winter.

Other resorts are being developed in the nearby area, and the slopes of the Grande-Moucherolle offer some outstanding summer walks.

The village of Valchevrière, which was destroyed in 1944, is now hidden under the shrubs and grass; it can be reached by a way of the cross which commemorates the Resistance fighters who lost their lives in the war.

Above, the Mont des Deux-Sœurs, in the Vercors massif, and the rather unusual spectacle of windmille in the snow. Facing, left and right, typical road and tunnel in the Vercors.

THE OISANS
AND THE ECRINS NATIONAL PARK

The Oisans consists for the most part of two enormous glaciary massifs, that of La Meige, which reaches its highest point opposite La Grave at 13,065 ft., and that of Les Ecrins, now a National Park, with the Pic d'Olan (11,740 ft.) and Mount Pelvoux (12,950 ft.). It is one of the biggest of the French national parks, with 230,000 protected acres. The Barre des Ecrins (13,455 ft.) lies between these two mountainous areas.

The confines of the Oisans are formed by two valleys: to the north, the Romanche, and to the south the Séveraisse, in Valgaudémar. In the middle, Vénéon Valley is served by a road which runs at a giddy height through Bourg-d'Arud and Saint-Christophe-en-Oisans to La Bérarde (5,625 ft.). From this out-of-the-way village hikers can climb the Tête de la Maye or work their way back up towards the Carrelet shelter and the Pilatte Glacier, which contains the source of the Vénéon.

If one enters the Oisans by the Romanche Valley, one should head straight for its middle section, at Bourg-d'Oisans, a small mountain village which makes a good starting point for touring the area. Downstream the Romanche Valley is irreparably polluted and overrun by industrial sprawl and hydroelectric facilities.

Bourg-d'Oisans also occurs at a crossroads, the most popular route being the one that leads to L'Alpe-d'Huez (6,100 ft.) an excellent skiing resort which is used even in the summer months, by skiers taking the runs on the Sarennes Glacier.

Other minor roads lead to a number of picturesque villages which are situated on terraces overlooking the massifs of Les Grandes-Rousses and Belledonne.

Beyond Bourg-d'Oisans the *route nationale* climbs up the Romanche valley towards two major passes: the Col du Lautaret and the Col du Galibier.

Chambon dam has formed a lake of some 310 acres. To the north is the old village of Besse, from which it is possible to take a trail up to the road leading to the Col de la Croix de Fer. Higher up again we come to La Grave, a favorite with mountain climbers. A 12th-century Romanesque church stands in the middle of a small cemetery which contains the remains of a number of victims of climbing accidents. From the oratory of Le Chazelet there is a superb panorama of the peaks and glaciers of the Meige.

At Villard-d'Arène the road leaves the river and climbs towards the Col du Lautaret and Monnetier-les-Bains, which is well situated in a fertile valley. Seasoned hikers, however, can reach Monnetier by going upstream along the Romanche from Villard-d'Arène past the chalets of L'Alpe and the Col d'Arsine, in a landscape ringed by boulders and pasturelands, against a background of the snow-capped peaks of the Meige, the Grande Ruine, the peaks of Neige-Cordier and of Chamoisières.

Besides being the most remarkable mountain area in Europe, after the Mont-Blanc massif, and offering mountain climbers an unusually varied choice of ascents, the Oisans is also, with its numerous trails and vantage points, one of the most beautiful Alpine regions in France.

Top, two of the glaciers of the Oisans. Left, view of the Écrins National Park and, right, view of the high valley of the Romanche.

TRIÈVES AND VALGAUDÉMAR
DEVOLUY AND CHAMPSAUR

A plateau, resting on the slopes of the Vercors and Mount Aiguille (6,880 ft.), an astonishing monolith crowned by a slab-like peak; and a valley pointing towards the sources of two rivers, the Bonne and the Séveraisse.

Mount Aiguille used to be known as the "inaccessible mountain"—until the day when, on the royal orders of Charles VII, a captain and ten of his men attempted the difficult ascent. They made it, by using rope ladders, and spent several days at the top.

The two major highways of the Alps cross the Trièves, one via the Col de Lus-la-Croix-Haute (3,600 ft.) and the other via Corps, which has a panoramic view of the Drac Valley and the Sautet dam. From Corps it is possible to visit the monastery of Notre-Dame-de-la-Salette, along a road which runs past sheer ravines. There is a hoselry to house pilgrims.

La Mure, further to the north, is a fine center for touring the valleys adjoining the western part of the gigantic Ecrins massif: Le Valbonnais, Le Valjouffrey—with La Chapelle-en-Valjouffrey, from which the "desert" can be reached along a narrow valley which climbs the course of the Bonne, at the foot of the Pic des Souffles, leading to the spectacular sight of the sheer rock faces of the Olan, in a most remarkable landscape.

Lower down, the Valgaudémar, with characteristic villages spread out along the Séveraisse, beneath grassy slopes and rockslides. The most interesting scenery at this point is provided by the waterfalls known as Le Casset and Le Voile de la Mariée (The Bride's Veil), and Lake Lauzon (7,200 ft.), opposite the glacial amphitheater of the massif.

Super-Devoluy, a recently built winter sports resort has served to bring the wild massif after which it is named to the attention of a wide public. It is located south of Trièves, between Lus-La-Croix-Haute and Gap. The limestone massif of the Dévoluy, which is largely arid and riddled with caves, does have a number of lush valleys with some old villages: Saint-Didier, at the mouth of the Souloise defile and Saint-Etienne-en-Dévoluy, just over two miles from the resort. Most of the accomodation in Super-Dévoluy consists of apartments bought on time payments—a formula which seems to be increasingly popular in the region.

The Col du Noyer (5,460 ft.) opens onto broad pasturelands and leads to the Champsaur, which comprises the upper Drac Valley. The road which runs through this valley is rightly famous as one of the most impressive in the region.

The Champsaur, with an average altitude of about 3,000 ft., enjoys a particularly warm climate, as a result of its southerly exposure. It also has abundant rainfall.

A winter sports resort has been built on the slopes of Mount Drouvet, above the village of Orcières, and is known as Orcières-Merlette. As at Super-Dévoluy, seasonal sales are very common, particularly to residents of Marseille.

Saint-Bonnet, not far from the Route Napoléon, is more favored by summer vacationers, who have plenty of walks and climbs at their disposal in the vicinity. The village itself is interesting, with its old brown roofs and the square belltower of its church.

Left, river and Alpine flora at the Col du Lautaret. Above, the Valgaudémar Corridor. Right, the Col du Lautaret, overall view of the pass.

BRIANÇONNAIS AND VALLOUISE
THE QUEYRAS AND THE UBAYE

Briançon, at 4,330 ft., is the highest town in Europe. It was once a fortified strongpoint. As the capital of the *escartons*—a group of neighboring communes,—it was fortified by Vauban after being ravaged by fire in 1692. The old town is still surrounded by its original ramparts and still has its own covered way, gates, citadels and church of Notre-Dame, which was also built from Vauban's plans. The façade of the church is set between two square belltowers. The Maison des Templiers (House of the Knights Templar), which is situated just opposite, is in the Renaissance style.

A modern section has sprung up at the foot of the old town. Briançon is also a spa and an excellent center from which to tour the Briançonnais and the upland areas around the Pelvoux and the Barre des Ecrins. Since it is so close to the skiing at Serre-Chevalier and Mont-Genèvre, and particularly on account of its sunny climate, it is very popular with winter vacationers.

La Vallouise consists of a number of valleys formed by rivers which flow into the Durance. Vallouise itself is a village which is well worth

a visit, with its 16th-century church.

Two tributaries of the Durance, the Guil and the Ubaye, flow accross these two regions.

From Briançon the Grande Route des Alpes takes one up the Col d'Izoard, at 7,740 ft., and along the comb of the Queyras. On the way down the road passes through the Casse Déserte, an astonishing rocky amphitheater in which huge boulders stand amidst the slopes strewn with mountainous debris. The Arvieux valley leads to Château-Queyras, whose 13th-century fortress has a commanding position overlooking the narrowest point of the Guil Valley. Downstream the road leads to Guillestre, at the top of a sheer gorge.

From Château-Queyras, via Molines-en-Queyras, another road takes us to Saint-Véran, the highest village in Europe, at 6,725 ft. Some recent construction has marred the beauty of this mountain village. Here there is snow for eight months of the year, with a brief summer during which the flowers all bloom and fade within a few weeks.

Beyond Mount Fort-Sancte, which can be reached by some rather difficult trails, is the high valley of the Ubaye, with several villages: Saint-Paul, Jausiers, from which the *barcelonnettes* used to sail for Mexico, in the quest for fortune! And last of all, in the low valley, Barcelonnette, which was founded by the counts of Provence, lies bathed in sunlight.

Left: Vallouise, the Briançon Dam and the ancient fortress of Château-Queyras; a view of Barcelonnette and the milestone which marks the top of the Col de l'Izoard. Above, the setting of Saint-Paul-sur-Ubaye. Below, the strange landscape of La Casse Déserte, on the road to l'Izoard.

THE PROVENCE ALPS
AND THE ROUTE NAPOLEON

From Grenoble, two major roads cross the Alpine massifs on their way to the Riviera. One proceeds via the pass of Lus-la-Croix-Haute, at 3,445 ft., and the other takes the Col Bayard, at 4,090 ft. They meet at Sisteron, the gateway to Alpine Provence. A regular bus service runs along this magnificent route across the Hautes-Alpes, the Alpes de Haute-Provence and the Alpes-Maritimes summer and winter, between Geneva and Nice, via Grenoble.

The two passes mark a climatic frontier. It is quite common, particularly in winter, to see the sky clear suddenly as the road enters the Buech Valley, after Lus, or as one begins the descent from the Col Bayard to Gap.

This second road, known as the Route Napoléon, joins the Durance downstream from Taillard —which produces a fine local white wine—at which point the Alpine landscape becomes distinctly more arid and rocky.

Sisteron, at the confluence of the Buech and the Durance, lies in the shadow of its fortress, the origins of which date back to the 12th century. The fortifications are from the time of Henri IV. The covered way can be reached by stairs interrupted by terraces from which there is a fine panoramic view over the town, the valley and, on the other side, the cliffs of La Baume.

The church of Notre-Dame, in the Provençal Romanesque style, is situated in the heart of the old town, with its narrow streets, tall houses and vaulted passage-ways.

Beyond Sisteron, the Route Napoléon moves on to Château-Arnoux and leaves the Durance Valley on its way to Digne. Here again we come across a Romanesque church with a Lombard portal and curious fountain whose limestone deposits are covered with an abundance of moss.

At Castellane the road crosses the valley of the Verdon. The town is built on the right bank of the river, at the foot of the famous Rock, which rises sheer from the valley floor for over 600 ft. At the top is the chapel of Notre-Dame-du-Roc, which can be reached by a steep path. The central square at the bottom of the rock, with its terrace cafes and hotels is typically Provençal. Some distance further on, in the old town, the church of Saint-Victor (2nd century) brings to mind the memory of its founders, the monks of the abbey of Saint-Victor of Marseille.

The road then climbs back up through a lush landscape to the hamlet of La Garde and the Col de Luens at 3,460 ft. After a number of gentle vales we come to a broad plateau through which a tributary of the Verdon, the river Artuby, flows. At the crossroads of the Logis du Pain, a road leads to Saint-Auban, a mountain village at the mouth of a wild rift. Another road leads to Comps-sur-Artuby and Draguignan.

Then, not far from the Col de Valferrière, in the direction of Caille and Andon, we reach L'Audibergue, a modest winter resort on the Cannes coast, in the midst of a desolate rocky plateau which stretches towards Thorenc and Gréolières-les-Neiges, a winter sports center which was built on a totally vacant site some twenty years ago, on the north slope of the Cheiron.

Top, view from the Route Napoléon (so named because the emperor passed this way on his return from Elba). Facing, the Lac de Saint-Apollinaire, in the Hautes-Alpes.

THE HIGH VALLEY
AND THE GORGES OF THE VERDON

La Foux d'Allos, a winter resort which was launched after the war, is very popular with skiers from the south of France, who can be sure of finding there, at 5,900 ft., a reliable snow cover for several months of the year. At 7,380 ft., the Col d'Allos, which is often closed in winter, links the Ubaye and Verdon valleys; the source of the Verdon is situated on the side of Séolane, near the pass.

While La Foux d'Allos is the favorite of winter sports enthusiasts, the high valley of the Verdon, in summer, provides many interesting walks and good places to stay. The high valley of the Verdon, which is open to the south and is **Below: a view of the Verdon Gorges; the small town of Sisteron and the mountain of La Baume (left); Moustiers-Sainte-Marie, which is famous for its ceramics (right).**

protected to the north by a succession of peaks of between 8,200 and 9,850 ft. (Séolane, 9,525 ft; the Trois-Evêches, 8,420 ft; Le Cernet, 9,915 ft; Le Pelat 10,015 ft.) combines the freshness of an Alpine region with the sky and the light one associates with Provence.

Allos, at 4,675 ft., is still very much a typical mountain village, with its wooden houses and their haylofts. Its altitude, the purity of its air, the charm of its climate and its larch forest make Allos a touring center much favored by mountain walkers and other nature lovers. The most attractive walk is the one around Lake Allos—an optional extra being the ascent of Mount Pelat (9,840 ft.), which is within the capacity of most walkers in reasonable condition. On a clear day there is a view as far as the Mediterranean, and, in the north, as the formidable peaks, between 3,280 and 4,920 ft. high, above the snow line. An ocean of rock, snow and forest...

There are other trips through the hamlets of

Seignus, Le Haut-Villard and the woods of La Vacheresse. The descent of the Verdon valley is also worthwhile. Here we come across the curious village of Colmars, hemmed in by defensive walls with loopholes and the gates of France and Savoy.

Further down we come to Beauvezer, Saint-André-des-Alpes, the large lake formed by the Castillon dam and then Castellane, where we rejoin the Route Napoléon. Castellane is the point of departure for the trip through the Verdon gorges, either via the corniche roads which run along the rim of the canyon, or, for sporting types, along the bottom of the gorges, on foot or by canoe. Because of engineering works upstream, however, this can be a dangerous walk, as the water level may rise suddenly.

There is hardly anything to match the Verdon Gorges in Europe: 28 miles long, a gash in the earth's surface 920 to nearly 1,500 ft. deep, and some splendid vantage points over a sheer drop: the Point Sublime and the Escalès belvedere.

THE VAR VALLEY:
FROM THE ALPS TO THE SEA

The Col de la Cayolle, at 7,630 ft., opens a valley parallel to that of the Verdon, the valley of the river Var, which flows through gorges and a generally rocky landscape on its way to the Mediterranean.

The pass lies between the peak of Sanguinière (8,530 ft) and Les Garrets (9,210 ft.). A stream formed from melting snow cascades down the lower slopes, but the source of the Var is lower down, in a meadow—a narrow strip of water which eventually flows into the Sanguinière torrent. After the rock-strewn slopes the road runs between pasturelands in the shadow of the Aiguilles de Pelens. At the hamlet of Estang there is an old chapel and some chalets with board roofs. Soon we come to the first gorges carved out by the river, and the first village, Entraunes, followed by Saint-Martin d'Entraunes, with its old church standing separately from its belltower and containing a fine altarpiece by François Bréa, of the 15th-century Nice school. The village is a mixture of Alpine and Provençal, combining mountain chalets and tall façades colored in the Italian manner.

Thereafter the valley broadens on its way to Guillaumes, the landmark of which is its ruined castle. It has many geraniums and rose-laurels, growing in arbors and terraces, and is surrounded by an amphitheater of dolomitic rocks, through which the road to Valberg and Péone passes.

The valley is then enclosed once again between slopes of reddish schist as it reaches the famous Daluis Gorges, a favorite with tourists making ther way to the Riviera.

An open gash has been cut through the mountains for some six miles, forming the most fantastic rock faces. The road runs along three hundred feet above the Var, through tunnels and under overhanging rocks, which are adorned in winter with icy stalactites.

Just after the gorges, the valley opens up again, as the Var spreads out over a gravel bed before meeting its tributary, the Coulomb, at Pont-de-Gueydan. Passing through the small town of Entrevaux, which was fortified by Vauban, and then Puget-Théniers and Touët-sur-Var, between steep mountains and through the Mescla Gorges, the Var—this section of which was once the frontier of Savoy—moves down to the Mediterranean along a broad valley. On the way it acquires the added volume of a number of tributaries: the Tinée, the Vésubie and, on the other bank, the Estéron, a picturesque valley with a number of high "perched villages"—Gillette, Bouyon and Roquesteron.

Valberg, the other side of Guillaumes, is a sunny winters-sports resort, but it is also, with its splendid forests of larch trees and its extensive views of the Provençal Alps, a particularly pleasant mountain touring center in summer. Beuil, just under four miles away, is an old mountain hamley with a 17th-century church and steep streets. Further to the north is the out-of-way village of Péone on the slopes of Mount Mounier (9,246 ft.), one of the highest peaks of the Alpes Maritimes.

An Alpine pasture, or *alpage*, in Haute-Provence. A curious sight: the Pénitents des Nuées. Right, the harvest at Villar-d'Arène and fields of lavender on the Valensole Plateau.

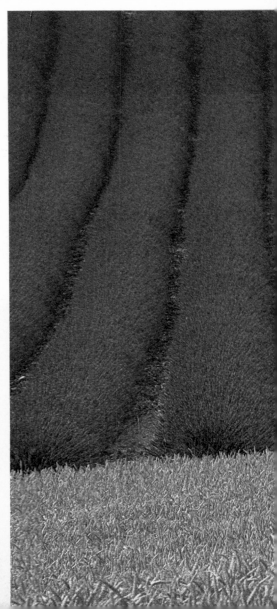

VALLEYS AND PLACES
IN THE ALPES MARITIMES

Whereas the Provençal Alps stretch out in ranges parallel to the sea, the Alpes Maritimes, from the Var to the Roya valleys, are at right angles to the Mediterranean.

Beuil, once the domain of the Grimaldis, situated at 4,756 ft., is linked to these valleys by winding roads leading to Guillaume and the Var, in one direction, and to Tinée and the Vésubie in the other.

In the south another road joins the Var near Touët, along the splendid Cians Gorges, which can be toured jointly with the Daluis Gorges. Eastwards, the road takes us through Roubion, an isolated village surrounded by ravines, to the Tinée Valley at Saint-Sauveur-de-Tinée.

The Tinée Valley is certainly the most interesting of all the valleys in the Nice hinterland. After the confluence with the Var, at the Mescla bridge, we enter a world of magnificent gorges, whose sheer walls tower over the road.

Although motorists tend as a rule to drive on without stopping to visit them, villages such as Bairols and Ilonse, on the right bank of the river, and Clans, surrounded by chestnut treets, and well endowed with medicinally valuable spring water, on the left bank, are perched so high up the mountainside that they provide sweeping views of the landscape below.

Saint-Sauveur-de-Tinée has a Romanesque church. Further on, the Valabres Gorges are located just before the village of Isola, where a new road leads off to the modern winter-sports complex of Isola-2000, complete with hotels and shops, at the foot of some fine upland slopes. The road then continues as far as the Col de la Lombarde (7,725 ft.) on the Italian border.

The road along the Tinée climbs the high valley in the direction of Saint-Etienne-de-Tinée (3,742 ft.), where two other roads meet, including the road to Auron (5,250 ft.), the best and most widely known of the ski resorts of the Alpes

Maritimes.

The other road climbs even higher to Saint-Dalmas-le-Selvage, isolated in its wild setting, and also to the Col de Restefonds and La Bonnette peak, at 9,185 ft., in a breathtaking landscape of rocky slopes and snowy mountain tops.

The Vésubie valley, to which we can return from Saint-Sauveur-de-Tinée via the Col Saint-Martin has a remarkable landscape of its own which includes the Boréon waterfall and some winter and summer resorts, such as La Colmiane, and Saint-Martin-Vésubie, respectively, which are very popular with the residents of Nice.

Lower down the valley, across from Saint-Jean-

la-Rivière, a road climbs boldly through magnificent olive groves as far as Utelle and the sanctuary of the Madonna of Utelle, a noted shrine from which there is a superb view of the Alpes Maritimes. The spot known as Frenchmen's Leap (Le Saut des Français) in the Vésubie Gorges is a reminder of the tragic episode in 1793 in which local Chouans threw the Republican soldiers over the edge into the abyss.

The famous "perched villages" on the most southerly slopes of the Alps, close to the Mediterranean; above, Castellar, and, right, a small town in the Vésubie Valley. Left, the setting of Auron, a winter-sports resort in the *département* of Alpes-Maritimes. Below, Alpine pastures in the region.

THE MERCANTOUR:
MOUNTAINS AND MARVELS

The Roya, the most easterly of the rivers in the Alpes Maritimes, flows from the frontier range, to the left of the Col de Tende, down to the Mediterranean at Ventimiglia in Italy.

This upper Roya valley was not returned to France until the adoption of the treaty of 1947. It had been granted to Italy in 1860, when Savoy and the County of Nice were attached to France, as a gesture of courtesy on the part of Napoleon to King Victor-Emmanuel, who was particularly fond of hunting in the Mercantour massif.

In this way, Tende and La Brigue, two very curious mountain hamlets, found themselves linked to Italy, and became French again 35 years ago. Tende is an important place on the road to the Piedmont Alps and Turin; it is also a point of departure for visits to the Mercantour region, where the peaks of Mount Clapier (9,990 ft.), Mount Bego (9,420 ft.) and the Grand Capelet (9,625 ft.) provide an admirable setting for the protected wildlife, the forests and the lakes of the Mercantour National Park.

The Mercantour park reaches as far as the confines of the upper Vésubie Valley, towards the Boréon and the Aution which, beyond the splendid Turini forest form a balcony from which the huge forests of the area may be surveyed.

Mercantour park also contains the astonishing Valley of Marvels. It can be reached from the Roya Valley along a small road which runs the length of the Minière Torrent and which can be used only by four-wheel drive vehicles.

The Vallée des Merveilles, which was discovered in the 18th century, is an out-of-the-way valley on the slopes of Mount Bego, where the rock faces are covered with thousands of carved inscriptions. Scholars have as yet proved unable to determine their origin or meaning. They consist of geometric figures and assorted patterns which are thought to date back to the bronze age or the iron age.

Late in the 19th century an English scholar became enthralled by the place and its mysteries, built a house for himself and lived there until his death.

The high valleys of the region consist of lush landscap and mountain springs and remote lakes, such as Lac Vert, and rocky slopes adorned by mountain flowers.

A narrow road climbs past the torrent from Saint-Dalmas-de-Tende and takes us to La Brigue, whose old church contains some fine paintings by the Bréa family. The Chapel of Notre-Dame-des-Fontaines, a little further on, also houses a number of remarkable frescoes. Mount Saccarel, (7,285 ft.) can be reached by a number of paths.

On our way downstream along the Roya we come to Fontan, ringed by mountains, and Saorge, clinging to the slopes from a dominant position overlooking the Roya Gorges. The church of the Madonne del Poggio, in the Romanesque style with a Lombard belltower, is situated next to a Franciscan monastery.

Further downstream we come to Breil-sur-Roya which is a curious place in that it is an international station, on French territory, between Coni and Ventimiglia—both of which are in Italy.

Three views of the Massif du Mercantour, close to the Riviera.

THE VAUDOIS ALPS

The very names of the Vaudois Alps—Tower, Head, Teeth, Point—give one an idea of the kind of wild, rugged peaks one might expect to find there. From the low-lying regions of the Rhone and Léman valleys, the ground rises steeply to forests and pasture-lands, above which are sheer rock faces and glaciers.

The best known of the massifs are the Diablerets (10,597 ft.), the Grand Muveran (10,010 ft.), the Rochers de Naye (6,700 ft.), the Tours d'Aï and the Dent de Jaman (6,152 ft.).

Deep in the valleys and on the slopes which are most exposed to the sun there is a succession of vineyards; it is hardly surprising, therefore, that the Festival of the Wine-Makers has been held at Vevey since 1797, once every twenty-five years. About six miles away is Montreux, now greatly

rejuvenated by some inspired town-planning, and definitely the liveliest resort in the area. For many years it was a favorite with the English aristocracy and the Grand-Dukes of Russia. Jean-Jacques Rousseau chose the village of Clarens, now a suburb of Montreux, as the setting for his *Nouvelle Héloïse.* Blessed by an exceedingly mild climate—hence the name Vaudois Riviera which is given to this stretch of the lake—Montreux in springtime is a delight to behold, as its terraced fields uphill from the lake are covered with narcissuses while the lakefront is ablaze with the blossom of almond and fig trees and magnolias. Montreux is well known on account of its festivals, which attract international attention: they include the televised festival of the *Rose d'Or,* in April, and the famous concerts which take place in September.

A few miles further on towards the end of the lake the famous Château de Chillon is a must for visitors: built on a rocky islet, it stands in a most picturesque setting, framed by the uniquely beautiful scenery of the lake, Montreux, the French shore and the Alps, with the prominent Dents du Midi.

The first fortress on this site was built in the 9th century to keep a tight watch over the route to

Italy via the Grand Saint-Bernard Pass. The dungeons of Chillon have repeatedly been used as a State prison. The most famous of the prisoners it has housed was François Bonivard, whom Byron immortalized in a deeply lyrical work, *The prisoner of Chillon.*

In the vicinity of Montreux, the Pléiades (4,462 ft.) make a delightful walk. It is possible to drive as far as Lally, and then walk on from there to the top, across fields and through woods. There is also a funicular railway to Lally from Blonay. There is a superb panoramic view of the lake, the Molard, the Dent de Jaman, the Rochers de Naye and the Mont-Blanc range. From Montreux it is possible to take the blue trains of the Montreux-Oberland-Bernois railroad (MOB) to reach the world-famous resort of Gstaad, where the Bernese Oberland meets the Vaudois Alps. In both summer and winter Gstaad is home to crowned heads, stars and other celebrities, including the family of

On the Swiss side of Lake Léman: Saint-Saphorin, Montreux, the Château de Chillon. Right, view of the mountains at the upstream end of the lake, a peak near Gstaad and the resort of Les Diablerets.

the ruling house of Monaco, Liz Taylor and Yehudi Menuhin, whose festival in June attracts large numbers of music lovers each year. Gstaad still has its sleighs, its Rolls-Royce which takes guests from the station to the Palace Hotel and its cosy atmosphere, all of which have made it a favorite with the rich and famous; but it is also popular with people who want excellent winter sports facilities and very good skiing—all of which it has.

There is a cog railway which runs from Montreux up to the Rochers de Naye. The resort of Les Diablerets, in the heart of the Vaudois Alps, has developed considerably in recent years. It can be reached by train from Aigle. The Diablerets Glacier, which is open from February to November, makes it possible for skiers to enjoy their sport during the summer months. Château-d'Oex, the chief administrative town of the Pays d'Enhaut, is typical of the family resorts to be found in the Vaudois Alps. Its Musée du Vieux-Pays d'Enhaut brings to life the history of this part of Switzerland, which belonged to the county of Gruyère, and then to the canton of Berne, before being attached to the canton of Vaud upon its entry into the Confederation in 1803.

THE VALAIS ALPS

As a result of the Grand St. Bernard and Simplon passes, the Rhône Valley, a broad furrow in the earth's crust which ranges from the Furka to Lake Léman, carries an immense amount of international traffic. The Rhône, which rises at 7,218 ft. in the glacier of the same name, crosses the Upper Valais, where a very colorful German dialect is spoken, runs along the Bois de Finges as far as Sierre, at which point the inhabitants of the Valais speak French, and then on down to the Lower Valais. The climate of the Rhône Valley is extraordinarily dry, with less than 24 inches of average annual precipitation.

After its confluence with the Dranse at Martigny, the Rhône turns sharply northwards. Martigny, with its dominant landmark, the round tower of the Bâtiaz and the ruins of its fortifications, is an international crossroads receiving converging traffic from the Grand St. Bernard and Simplon passes, as well as from the Forclaz, which leads into France and Chamonix.

A road with plenty of hairpin bends leads from Orsières to Champex, in the Vall Ferret. Champex is a delightful resort, set in a deep wooded bend in the valley, which, thanks to its small lake, combines the charms of beach and boating to those of the mountain. The snow-capped peaks of the two Combins (Combin de Corbassière and Grand Combin) can be seen from Champex.

Let us now return to the Entremont Valley and the road to the Grand St. Bernard, which runs for

Above, scene in the Vallée de la Sage, Haut-Valais. Bottom, Zermatt at night and the Matterhorn. Right, the Lac Bleu, in the Val d'Hérens and a hiking trail near Zermatt.

twenty-seven miles. The hospitality of the monks of the Grand St. Bernard and their famous dogs have been a tradition which has lasted since the 11th century. Large numbers of tourists making a sort of historical pilgrimage are also attracted to this wild and desolate area each year, following the route taken by Napoleon's armies in 1800. In the light of the very heavy road traffic between the Rhône and Aosta valleys, Switzerland and Italy have jointly completed the toll tunnel of the Grand St. Bernard, which brings Basel to within 270 miles of Turin.

Sion, the capital of the Valais, can be seen from a long way off because of its two prominent hills: Valère and Tourbillon. The structures of top of them are respectively the church of Notre-Dame de Valère and the ruined Tourbillon Castle.

The Val d'Hérens, one of the most picturesque valleys in the French-speaking Valais, leads from Sion to Les Haudères, a town in which, like Evolène, traditional costumes are still to be seen! Another side valley with which experienced mountain climbers are all doubtless familiar is the Val d'Anniviers, which can be reached from Sierre; the highest village in Europe, Chandolin (6,352 ft.) is located in this valley.

A unique resort, famous throughout the world —and rightly so!— is Zermatt, which can be reached by narrow-gauge railroad from Visp; many motorists leave their cars at Täsch, the penultimate station on the line. Zermatt is a special place, apart from the rest of the world: for one thing, the internal combustion engine is banned there, and, of course, it also has the incomparable Matterhorn! In 1865, the awesomely beautiful peak took the lives of four members of the climbing party of the English alpinist Edward Whymper, just after they had completed the first ascent of the mountain — the first, alas, of many such tragedies.

THE BERNESE OBERLAND / 1.

With its innumerable natural "sights" and the excellent facilities and terrain it offers the practitioners of alpine sports, the Bernese Oberland, which has the largest share of the Swiss Alps after the Valais and the Grisons, has been the most popular mountain area in the world, ever since the beginning of the age of modern tourism. Its picturesque houses, its Swiss-German dialects, its legends and its literature vary from one valley to the next. And the famous trio of the Eiger, the Mönch and the Jungfrau, with their eternal snow and towering peaks, are forever engraved in the history of mountain climbing.

The charming town of Thun, on the shores of the lake of that name, is the starting point for trips into the surrounding area. The road runs along the lake as far as Interlaken, via Oberhofen, with its famous 12th-century castle. Between Oberhofen and Merligen there is a superb walk along the lake, at its sunniest and most flowery point. Further on the road cuts its way through, corniche-style, and the shores of the lake become steeper and more deserted, until the descent into Interlaken begins, half a mile after Beatenbucht (where you can take the quaint small red funicular

Right, in the heart of the Fribourg Alps, Le Moléson. Bottom, Spiez on Lake Thun and Brienz. Right, Interlaken, in the heart of the Bernese Oberland, and the Wetterhorn, which towers over Grindelwald. Following pages: the three "giants" of the Bernese Alps and the small town of Mürren: the Eiger, the Moench and famous Jungfrau.

railway up to the Beatenberg).

Although less scenic and less sunny than Lake Thun, Lake Brienz is the least polluted in Switzerland! It is possible to go swimming in its green and invigorating waters: while the attraction of the charming village of Brienz is its amusing wooden sculptures.

Interlaken, which was a high-society metropolis at the beginning of the century, still has something of the feel of a capital about it during the lively summer months. Its name means "between the lakes"—the lakes being those of Thun and Brienz. The famous Höheweg Promenade, with lawns and flower beds on one side and a row of exceedingly grand hotels on the other, is a truly impressive boulevard. There are countless trips which can be made from Interlaken—on foot, by car, by cable car and even in a horse-drawn cab! And for those tourists who are none too anxious to venture far into the Jungfrau massif, the Schynige Platte, which can be reached by cog railway, is a remarkable vantage point with a fine alpine garden and a hotel with a panoramic terrace.

Grindelwald, the famous "village of the glaciers", is the place where winter sports, which are so popular nowadays, originally started. In 1888 one hotel stayed open all winter long, its guests devoting their time to sleigh-rides, skating or curling. It was in Grindelwald again, in 1891, that an Englishman was the first to put on skis, and that, in or around 1895, the first winter ascents of the Jungfrau and other peaks were made.

The setting is unforgettable: meadows dotted with fruit trees or maple trees, facing a majestic rocky barrier which ranges from the Wetterhorn to the Eiger. The Jungfraujoch (11,400 ft.) may be reached from Grindelwald; it is unique among the resorts of Europe, being divided as it is between the hotel trade and scientific research, and on account of its remarkable view, which extends all the way as far as the Vosges and the Black Forest.

THE BERNESE OBERLAND / 2 .

The Jungfrau massif, in the heart of the Bernese Oberland, was recognized at a very early date as an ideal of Alpine beauty. "Its very special geology—sheer rock faces consisting of limestone coated with crystalline rocks protecting the summits—has been responsible for that characteristic appearance of icy rock, which can be seen from a great distance".

In fine weather the rail trip to the Jungfrau, for which one should allow a whole day, is absolutely unique. The train leaves Interlaken and reaches Grindelwald, after passing through one of the most typical resorts in the Bernese Oberland, Wengen (4,167 ft.), the Kleine-Scheidegg (6,762 ft.) which is very popular with skiers, the beginning of the Eiger glacier and the Jungfraujoch (see above). Any visitor who wishes to form an idea of the real Switzerland simply cannot afford to miss this trip !

Nowadays the St. Gotthard—rail or road— is an important crossing between central German Switzerland and the Ticino, besides being an international route. The tunnel, which was recently opened for road traffic, provides some relief for this north-south axis, which is particularly heavily traveled in summer. Travelers coming from the Bernese Oberland can get to the St. Gotthard via the Susten or Furka passes, which will enable them to enjoy the view of the famous Rhône Glacier.

From Gletsch (5,778 ft.) the road to the Furka takes the visitor to the edge of the glacier, to the Hôtel Belvédère. This famous side-trip shows the tourist the Grotto of Ice, the walls of which reflect a bluish light, and also the imposing panorama of the Bernese and Valais Alps.

We should note in passing that, since the middle of the last century, there has been a general shrinking of the glaciers. About a hundred years ago, for example, the Rhône glacier used to stretch all the way down to the valley, near Gletsch. "The glacier has since then lost a great deal of ground. Its tongue hangs rather pathetically from the top of the slope between the Grimsel and Furka passes, and is now reduced to a length of 5 1/2 miles and a surface area of seven square miles."

The sources of the Rhine are double, as the largest river in Northwest Europe consists, to begin with, of two headstreams: the Vorderrhein, which rises in the Oberalp, and the Hinterrhein, which flows from the Adula massif and joins its brother at Reichenau after cascading down through the famous Via Mala Gorges. The most spectacular part of the massif of the sources of the Rhine is near the village of Hinterrhein, as it is here that the huge Zapportgletscher and the Rheinquellhorn glacier are to be seen.

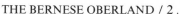

In the Bernese Oberland. Above, views of Wengen, at the foot of the Jungfrau, and the Sustenpass Glacier. Left, coming back from upland pastures. Right, view of the imposing Rhône Glacier.

beauty and of fierce, harsh grandeur.

Luzern, with its ancient wooden bridge, stone lion, Gletschergarten and well preserved old town, is one of the most attractive cities in Switzerland.

From Luzern to Altdorf the roads winds its way through a landscape dotted with walnut and fruit trees, following the ramifications of Lake Luzern and Lake Küssnacht, and climbing the reddish rocky spurs of the Rigi. It passes close to a little sanctuary built in memory of Queen Astrid, who died in a car crash at this spot on 29 August 1936. Küssnacht and Weggis are delightful places to stay. The Hohle Gasse ("hollow way") is situated almost two miles from Küssnacht: it was here that William Tell killed the bailiff Gessler. Vitznau, Gersau and Brunnen are pleasant vacation places with comfortable hotels. From Brunnen to Flüelen the road runs along the romantic shores of Lake Uri, a real deepwater fjord, noted for the famous Axenstrasse, whose opensided gallery has been replaced by a tunnel. This stretch of road is one of the most famous in the route to the St. Gotthard, and one of the most heavily traveled in Switzerland!

The chapel of Tell, which stands alone on the shores of Lake Uri, is an interesting place of pilgrimage, for those who are not deterred by a very steep path.

After this side-trip we return to the road to Altdorf, whose houses will soon come into sight.

The Rigi, at an altitude of 5,896 ft., has been famous since the middle of the 19th century for its highest point, the Rigi-Kulm. There used to be a tradition whereby one had to spend the night on the summit awaiting daybreak — an experience which was the apotheosis of a trip for Switzerland for those sensitive —and hardy— enough to per-

THE GLARON ALPS

The Klausen Pass (6,391 ft.) links the Bernese Oberland to the Glaron Alps, starting with the small town of Altdorf, at the eastern end of the Vierwaldstättersee. The main summits of the Glaron Alps are the Tödi (11,877 ft.), the Hausstock (10,360 ft), and the Mürtschenstock (8,009 ft.). All of them look down over the valley of the Linth which makes up the canton of Glaris.

The famous Rütli Meadow, the cradle of the Swiss Confederation, lies above the lake of the Four Cantons (Vierwaldstättersee). It was here, in 1291, that the inhabitants of the Austrian fiefs of Uri, Schwyz and Unterwald took the historic oath of Rütli, which opened up for them an era of liberty. This is William Tell country; the drama which Schiller wrote on the subject ranks as one of the masterpieces of German literature.

The lake, with its irregular shape and very steep slopes, is a gem in the heart of Switzerland. Any visitor who takes the steamer trip on its dark green waters comes away with an impression of

ceive it. The ascent is by cog railway from Arth-Goldau or Vitznau. The view of the Bernese and Glaron Alps is quite majestic.

Glaris, the capital of the canton of the same name, is well known, *inter alia,* for its *Landsgemeinde* (popular voting by a show of hands) and for its cotton and carpet industries. The printed calicoes of Glaris, in the 19th century, swamped the market, and even today the craftsmen of Glaris remain masters in the technique of printing.

This page: Brunnen and the Rütli; view of Luzern; the chapel built in memory of William Tell, near Küssnacht. Right, Mont Pilate and the Lake of the Four Cantons, with, in the middle, the Bürgenstock and, left, the Rigi.

THE GRISONS

The canton of the Grisons has three river basins: the Rhine, which flows into the North Sea, the Inn, which joins the Danube on its way to the Black Sea and the Ticino, a tributary of the Po, which flows into the Mediterranean. The languages spoken there are Italian, German and Romansch. Under the Romans, and during the Middle Ages, when it was known as Rhetia, the Grisons monopolized virtually all the Alpine traffic, through the Julier and Septimer passes on the Upper Route (the latter of these has now been completely abandoned) and the Splügen Pass on the Lower Route. The upper valley of the Hinterrhein, which begins in the vicinity of Splügen, has a number of interesting sights: the Roffla Gorges, which are nearly a thousand feet long, the famous Via Mala Gorges, which pass between awesome schist cliffs, and the village of Zillis, which is noted for its Romanesque church. The ceiling of this building dates from the 12th century and consists of 153 square panels which illustrate the mastery of the illuminator of manuscripts, reproducing, among others, scenes from the Apocalypse, the Last Judgment and the life of Christ.

The upper valley of the Vorderrhein, which flows down from the Oberalp, passes through Disentis, the small capital of the upper valleys of the Grisons Oberland which were colonized in the Middle Ages by the monks of Saint Benedict. The white abbey of Disentis can be seen in the distance as one descends the Lukmanier Pass. It is one of the oldest monastic foundations in Switzerland, having been founded in the 8th century. The abbey church is a major Baroque sanctuary, flanked by bulbous belltowers, which was restored in the 19th century after the abbey had been burnt down by French troops in 1799.

The resort of Flims, somewhat lower down, with its small Lake Cauma, which is kept at a mild temperature by hot underground springs, is much in demand, both winter and summer.

The Via Mala was famous long before the novelist John Knittel made a best-seller based on it: throughout the centuries this passage, which for half of its 5½ miles runs along the bottom of gorges, was the principal obstacle to the development of traffic on the Lower Route. The Via Mala itself is crossed by four bridges. Those wishing a fuller view of this remarkable spectacle may, from April to November, go down to the galleries which are much closer to the Rhine.

The Grisons are full of resorts which are as attractive in summer as they are in winter. Arosa (5,906 ft.) is one of the most elegant of these. It may be reached from Chur, the administrative seat of the canton, along a high and winding corniche road about twenty miles long. The resort is situated in the upper basin of the Schanfigg, in the Plessur Valley. With its record-breaking amounts of sunshine, Arosa lends itself well to relaxation and sports.

Davos (5,128 ft.), a famous health resort with a fine southerly exposure, is sheltered from the winds and is quite as sunny as Arosa. It is a paradise for skiing, sleigh-riding and skating, with excellent and well maintained facilities. These resorts are set in an attractive Alpine lanscape dotted with small lakes.

Left, the Rhine near Splügen, in the canton of Les Grisons, and one of the villages of the Lower Valley. Right, peasant house in the Grisons, view of Arosa and cowherds from Appenzell in period costumes.

ENGADINE

Engadine and its landscapes, which has been praised by the greatest names of European literature, uplift the soul and fill it with poetry. Upper Engadine, where the Inn has its source, is noted for its very dry climate; because the air, at the area's average altitude of 4,920 ft., is very rarified, solar radiation is unusually strong, particularly in winter. The typical Engadine houses, which remind one very much of Andalusia, and combine a rustic and a artistic charm, are truly wonderful. The best place to see them is at Zuoz, near St. Moritz.

St. Moritz, one of the most famous Swiss mountain resorts, both winter and summer, enjoys worldwide renown. Movie and show-business stars make a point of being seen there, while magnates and tycoons own chalets there and meet at the bars of the lavish hotels such as the Suvretta. St. Moritz Dorf has the oldest skiing school in the world (1927), whereas St. Moritz Bad takes pride in its thermal springs, whose curative virtues date back to the end of the Bronze Age! The Engadine Museum and the museum devoted to the works of the painter Segantini are worth a visit. Besides the high society side of life at St. Moritz, there is a great deal of racing—on toboggans, on horseback across the frozen lake, on sleighs, etc.

Lower Engadine, which is much more enclosed, is known mainly for its resorts of Tarasp, with its medieval castle, Scuol and Vulpera. In actual fact, Vulpera consists only of four hotels situated on a terrace of the wooded slope of the valley, in the

midst of magnificent flower beds. It is the most elegant resort in Lower Engadine.

It is useful to remember that visits to the Swiss National Park, a nature reserve of 40,000 acres, kept safe from human meddling, involve passing through the large Engadine village of Zernez. Anyone concerned with the need to protect our natural heritage will be delighted to see the rich variety of fauna and flora which is being so well cared for in this park.

The Bernina massif can be reached by taking the road which goes from St. Moritz, to Tirano, in the Tyrol. Although road traffic across the Bernina Pass is often blocked by deep snow from April to October, it is possible to get through by rail, on the highest railroad in Europe, all the year round. The Chünetta Belvedere (6,834 ft.) provides visitors with a majestic view of a huge amphitheater of glaciers. After the Bernina Pass the road descends to Poschiavo, where the atmosphere is definitely that of a town south of the Alps, indeed of one which is only twelve miles or so from the Italian border.

Left, the deep blue waters of Lake Sils, in Engadine, and the famous resorts of Saint-Moritz and Davos. Above, Lake Poschiavo; facing, the Bernina massif.

THE TICINO

Liberi e Svizzeri —free and Swiss— is the motto of the inhabitants of the Ticino. This canton in the southern Alps differs totally, by virtue of its geography, architecture, climate and mentality, from the rest of Switzerland. In a sense its attraction lies in this feature. Tourist arriving from the St. Gotthard travel down the valley of the Ticino, the upper stretches of which are called Léventine, from Airolo to Bellinzone, the administrative capital of the canton, and then further south to Locarno, on the shores of Lake Maggiore.

While Lake Lugano is almost entirely within the Ticino, Lake Maggiore on the other hand, is to a large extent in Italian territory. A section of it does, however, extend as far as Ascona and Locarno, treating its inhabitants to a more southern form of vegetation: next to the palm trees, hortensias and magnolias can be seen in bloom as early as March, and it is not unusual for camelias to flower towards the end of January!

Lake Lugano, which is smaller than lakes Maggiore and Como, is framed by very steep mountains covered with olive and chestnut trees. The dominant local landmark is the Monte San Salvatore, which one can ascend by funicular to enjoy an admirable view of the lake, as well as the Bernese and Valais Alps. Mount Bré, with its sunny terraces and its numerous walks, is another famous vantage point above Lake Lugano. Locarno, which has the benefits of a privileged climate, lies within a sunny bay on Lake Maggiore on the delta formed by the Maggia River. The town's historical monument is the Visconti Castle, with its archeological museum and museum of contemporary art. Locarno's main attraction, however, is certainly the Maddona del Sasso, a famous sanctuary perched at the top of a wooded spur, which can be reached either by road or by funicular from Locarno station. The nearby town of Ascona, much prized by painters, has a great deal to offer tourists. For those who prefer the picturesque traits of the typically Ticinese villages, the Centovalli, with their little train which runs from Locarno to Domodossola, have managed to remain exceedingly romantic. Lugano, known as the Queen of the Ceresio, lavishes countless celebrations, festivals and entertainments on its visitors, who can enjoy the beach, tennis, golf, horseback riding, boating and the casino. It has a delightful municipal park on the shore of the lake.

Gandria and Morcote, just along the lake towards Lake Como certainly deserve a visit, as they are among the most poetic places in the area.

Italian Switzerland is crossed by numerous valleys where life is still hard: the lake region is the only area where tourism has really developed — and there it has developed perhaps to excess, in recent years, with the German Swiss and the Germans spearheading these peaceful invaders! They keep coming because they realize that the unique beauty of the canton and the charm of its people make the Ticino an unforgettable vacation region.

More views of the Swiss Alps, but in a different light—that of the Ticino. Below, the setting of Locarno, and, right, three views of Lake Lugano.

THE BAVARIAN PASSES

The lion and the lighthouse at the end of the Lindau roadsteads are symbols of the lakes and the Alps of Germany. It is curious that the starting point of the German Alpine route should be this town built on an island on Lake Constance, the "Swabian sea", linked to the mainland by a road bridge and a long causeway.

From a shady vantage point in this charming tourist center you can make out the bluish outline of the Swiss and Bavarian Alps.

The approach to the mountains themselves passes through a gentle landscape of orchards and wooded foothills. Oberstaufen is a charming market town in the Allgäu, where the highest peak, the Staufen, does not exceed 3,385 ft. Nonetheless, it offers skiers fine and almost permanently snow-covered slopes. From this natural belvedere of the pre-Alps and the Paradies, at a wide bend in the road, it is possible to enjoy a sweeping panorama of the Appenzell Alps in Switzerland.

The road to the Oberjoch Pass has a more Alpine look about it. Charming resorts such as Hindenland and Bad Oberdorf on the Hochvogel (8,505 ft.) offer visitors a broad variety of delights. As well as walking trips in the nearby mountains and skiing in winter, there are the benefits of hydrotherapy at the famous mineral springs there. Not far from Hindenlang is the start of the famous "ascent with 106 bends", which allows unimpeded views of the peaks of the limestone Alps of the Allgäu. Kanzel is a convenient place from which to enjoy a good view of the Ostrach Valley, to the south, in the direction of the Nebelhorn (7,295 ft.)

You can reach the summit of this mountain near Oberstdorf by means of a large cable car and a chair lift. On the horizon it is possible to see the

Santis and the Zugspitze, while in the foreground is the sharp outline of the Hochvogel, the Gross Krottenkopf and the Urbeleskarspitze.

Oberstdorf is an internationally famous resort which can satisfy even the most demanding of tourists. The Alpine valleys provide climbers with some fine outings, while tourists and hikers sometimes have a hard time deciding which of the many excellent routes to take. Skiers at all levels of competence have huge fields of snow on which to practise. A huge ski jump, a skating rink and cable cars all add to the winter season's enjoyments.

Further north, as we rejoin the German Alpine

route, we come to Nesselwang, which has a typically Alpine look, with its steeple standing out against the Sauling and the Zugspitze. Pfronten is a resort whose houses are spread out over some 2 1/2 miles of wild and extremely rugged mountain scenery. Louis II of Bavaria contemplated building a huge neo-feudal structure on the site of a ruin. Thanks to the Breitenberg cable car, skiing dominates the huge slopes of the Hochalpe and in summer it is easy to go up to the Aggenstein.

Fussen is a small busy town divided by the river Lech, which flows thunderously into a narrow gorge some quarter of a mile from the town. Without a doubt, this town owes its popularity with summer visitors to its proximity to the famous royal castles. The town itself does, however, have some Baroque buildings and works of art which merit our attention. The parish church houses the relics of St. Magnus, patron saint of the Allgäu, and in the ancient abbey built on the site of his hermitage, there is an interesting painting of the Dance of Death and a Gothic group depicting St. Anne, the Virgin and the infant Jesus.

Left, entrance to the harbor and ancient tower at Lindau. Above, landscape in the Allgäu (in the background, the Tannheim Mountains). Right, view of the area around Füssen.

THE ROYAL BAVARIAN CASTLES

Hohenschwangau Castle was built between 1832 and 1936 in the midst of wild and beautiful scenery near the Alpsee, which lies below the steep slopes of the Sauling. Maximilian II of Bavaria had it built on a spur which had previously accomodated the ruins of a fortress of the Guelphs and the Staufens. In this impressive pseudo-Gothic residence Louis II spent his boyhood with his mother, Queen Marie. Swans figure frequently even in the name of the castle itself (*schwan*—swan). However, an even more obsessive image is that of the spirit of the temperamental, rather mad king himself. The ceiling of his bedroom features the canopy of heaven with twinkling stars. Louis II dreamed here of the castle he was having built nearby. Another sensitive guest at Hohenschwangau was Richard Wagner, who stayed there in 1865. In the music room you can find mementoes of this stay and of the high esteem in which the king held him.

From the window at Hohenschwangau, where Louis II watched the work at Neuschwanstein you can catch a glimpse of the castle—a romantic, fairy-tale sight. The great ivory-hued castle is impressive, yet at the same time delicate, with its towers, turrets and pinnacles. It rises up on a wooded promontory overlooking the dark waters of the lake. All around there is the quiet of the mountains and forests, the mists on the water which make one feel that the whole place could be a theater set rather than a real princely residence. Is there not some truth, after all, in the assertion that the man who designed it was a set designer rather than an architect? Louis II was in residence for only 102 days—long enough, however, to be captivated by the weird atmosphere in the stalactite caves, so strongly reminiscent of Tannhauser and Venus, the huge room where the music of Lohengrin was played, and the sumptuous, unfinished throne room. Painted and coffered paneled ceilings, gilding and numerous chandeliers in the Singers' Hall all bear witness to the state of madness in which the prince lived. Louis was found drowned in Lake Starnberg three days after being overthrown by government order, on 10 June 1886.

Further east in the Ammergau Alps, Louis II had the rococo castle at Lindenhof built between 1874 and 1879, with a level of ostentation matched only by Versailles. The ingeniously designed grounds, with their waterfalls, fountains and terraces, all in a beautiful Alpine setting, make a genuinely captivating impression.

The famous castles of Ludwig II, in the heart of the Bavarian Alps: Neuschwanstein (below); Hohenschwangau (right, with surrounding landscape and from close up); Linderhof (bottom right).

COLORFUL VILLAGES
AND SLENDID LAKES

In the lower foothills of the Ammergau Alps to the north, we come across the most representative example of rococo architecture in all of Bavaria— the church at Wies. Built by Dominique Zimmermann in 1746, this economically designed church has an oval cupola. Stucco, gilt, woodcarvings, frescoes and golden statues stand out tastefully against the whitewashed walls.

Another feature of Bavarian architecture greets the visitor to Oberammagau, a small bright town 2,790 ft. up in a wooded basin in the mountains. The houses all along the streets are covered with painted frescoes giving the place a theatrical appearance. The town owes its fame, however, to the stunning Passion Play which is performed by the townspeople. In 1632, the woodcarvers (whose craft still thrives today) vowed to perform the Passion Play every ten years for the rest of time if the village was spared from the plague. This came to pass, and ever since then almost a thousand adults and more than 250 children have kept the tradition alive in this beautiful village setting.

From the top of the Wank (5,840 ft.) you can see the Garmisch Partenkirchen Valley. Behind it is the Wetterstein and the massive Zugspitze, the highest mountain in Germany, at 9,730 ft. Although Garmisch and Partenkirchen jointly form a major health and winter sports resort, they have kept their original charm with parts of the town retaining painted façades and balconies decorated with flowers. The old church contains 14th— and 15th-century murals. Traditions are kept alive by the wearing of the national costume and the men

still smoke long china pipes.

The construction of unparalleled sports facilities for the 1936 Olympic Games assured Garmisch Partenkirchen of its place as a great resort. Its attractions include a competition ski jump, an Olympic skiing stadium and an ice rink with a surface of one acre. Major competitive events are held there, including the famous "Kandahar". A large choice of ski runs are available for amateurs, from the resort itself, at 2,360 ft., up to the snow

fields on the Zugspitzplatt, not to mention bobsleighing, curling and tobogganing.

Mittenwald is a tiny town on the border with Austria, which Goethe called "a living picture book". The silhouettes of its richly painted houses and its church tower, entirely covered with frescoes, are set against the backdrop of the Karwendel range. There are plenty of steep walks and climbs here and on the Wetterstein, while bathing places are at hand in the surrounding lakes. Violin making has prospered here since 1684 when Matthew Klotz returned from learning his craft at Cremone to found a workshop.

The abundance of lakes—almost two hundred in all—is one of the attractions of Bavaria. There is the Walchensee, with its wild scenery and then, some distance down the twisting road to the Kochelsee we come to the blue waters of the Tegernsee, with charming blossom-laden villages all along its shores, and the enchanting Schliersee.

Left, the Geroldsee and a view of the Garmisch-Partenkirchen. Right decorated house at Oberammergau. Below, the Walchensee.

FROM THE WENDELSTEIN
TO THE CHIEMSEE

Munich is set so deep in the Bavarian countryside that even in clear weather nothing can be seen of the city itself, on the horizon—only the soft blurred outline of the Alpine peaks. Although this city is one of the biggest in Germany it has few of the characteristics of an Alpine metropolis, but as it is the capital of Bavaria and the pride of the Bavarian people, it deserves a mention here. Lovers of the Alps are drawn to Munich by the wealth of its architecture, works of art and folklore. Visitors should certainly not miss the Liebfrauenkirche, with its two characteristic towers, from which the street descends into the medieval section of the town which, besides being picturesque, is still very much alive. Today the expressway which links Munich to Salzburg makes the heart of the Alpine countryside easily accessible.

The Wendelstein (6,030 ft.), situated between the Schiersee and the Inn Valley is a popular place for outings. A cog railway goes as far as 5,640 ft. From there on, footbridges perilously fixed to the rock face take you to the summit. Great mountain ranges stretch out as far as the eye can see—the Chiemgau massif, the impressive Berchtesgaden Alps, the bold outlines of the Kairsergebirge and the Hohe Tauern. On top of this prodigious vantage point there is a solar observatory and an 18th-century chapel built by pious Bavarians.

Bayrichzell, situated in a deep valley near the Wendelstein, is a resort with first class hotels and sports facilities.

The Inn Valley has two quite distinct features. To the south it is wild, narrow and steeply banked with the high Kaisergebirge peaks as a backdrop. Towards the north the valley widens before returning to the open countryside. There it shelters some charming villages, with the tall, slender spires which are so typically Bavarian.

Some distance beyond the Inn Valley, the Chiemsee spreads out its blue waters opposite the continuous line of the Alps on the horizon. Watersports enthusiasts frequent the smart resorts which are dotted along the lakeshore. This lake,

the biggest in Bavaria, is sometimes called the Bavarian Sea. On one of the islands in the lake, the Herreninsel, stands Louis II of Bavaria's "folly"—a perfect copy of the Palace of Versailles. This work, which was begun in 1878, was interrupted by the death of the king. In summer, spectacular concerts are held there. On another

island, Fraueninsel, there is a Benedictine monastery in the style of churches of the 13th to 15th centuries.

A delightful valley running along the Tyroler Ache leads from the shores of the Chiemsee to Marquartstein, an attractive resort at the foot of the Chiemgau mountain range. Further south there are opulent houses with characteristic pinnacle-turreted balconies at Reit im Winkl, set against a backdrop of the Zahmer Kaiser and Wilder Kaiser. At the opening of the valleys stretching along the Chiemgau Alps in the Traun Blanche Valley lies Ruhpolding, a fascinating summer resort with dainty flower-bedecked houses, a delightful Enchanted Forest, waterfalls, and, especially if one takes the Rauschberg cable car, a wide variety of walks.

Left, a view of the Chiemgau; the narrow-gauge train on the Chiemsee, and, in the middle of the Lake, the Fraueninsel. Above, the Wendelstein. Right, returning from Alpine pastures in Bavaria.

CITIES OF SALT

Bad Reichenhall (*hall:*salt) is situated at the entrance to this Bavarian enclave, which is so curiously embedded in Austrian territory. Like its neighbor, Berchtesgaden, it owes its prosperity to the salt which had been mined here since Celtic times from the most abundant sources in the whole of Europe. There natural waters, like those at Berchtesgaden, are treated at the source in an ultra-modern salt works and supply some 70,000 metric tons of domestic salt. The salt works, which were built in 1834 in the neo-Gothic style then in vogue, have some impressive machinery for the visitor to admire.

Nevertheless, although the extraction of salt may have been its original function, Bad Reichenhall is nowadays, above all else, an elegant spa resort, with a slightly seedy charm. Situated at an altitude of 1,540 ft., by the mouth of the last of the Saalach Gorges, this delightful flowery town specializes in the treatment of respiratory ailments. The 12th-century church of Saint Zenon, like its namesake in Verona, shows a distinct Lombard influence.

Tucked into the rocky escarpments of the Reiteralpe, from Bad Reichenhall to Berchtesgaden there is a series of small wooded valleys, green pastures dotted with dark wooden chalets with flowerstrewn balconies. Occasionally one catches glimpses of some wonderful views of the Vlaueis, which is so highly esteemed by lovers of the Alps, and the familiar outline of the Watzmann at Berchtesgaden.

After the last gorges, we come to the delightful little town of Berchtesgaden, situated in its own river basin, surrounded by the impressive ranges of the Watzmann, the Steinernes Meer and the Hagengebirge. It owes its origins to the development of an Augustine priory, of which all that now remains is the structure known as the Castle, with a fine 13th-century cloister. It contains some interesting collections of 15th–and 16th-century wood carvings. The collegiate church shows signs of Lombard influence.

Hitler established his "domain" on the nearby Obersalzberg. The Allies razed the Beighof and its buildings to the ground, and all that remains are some foundations. The Eagle's Net at the top of the Kehlstein (6,015 ft.), which Hitler visited only about a dozen times has become a pleasant mountain inn. From it you can enjoy an incomparable view of the peaks all around as far as the pre-Alps of Salzburg and Dachstein.

The salt mines are another attraction for visitors, who tour them dressed as miners. The trip through the tunnel is made in a small train followed by a ride on a float across an illuminated underground lake.

The nearby Königsee provides one of the most romantic images of Upper Bavaria. Against a backdrop of snowy peaks, the tribolate shape of Saint Bartholomew's Chapel, formerly a hunting lodge in the 17th century, is reflected through a halo of delicate mist in the waters of the lake, into which the rock faces of the Watzmann and the Steinernes Meer plunge steeply.

Berchtesgaden: left and above the beautiful church of Maria Gern, a place of pilgrimage. Below, the chapel of Saint Bartholomew, on the Königsee.

THE VORARLBERG

For thousands of years the Vorarlberg has been a place of transit, but it managed to keep its traditions and its beautiful regional costumes until the last few decades. With the change from villages to resorts the ancestral costume disappeared altogether, and only the occasional folklore festivals and the interesting museums keep their memory alive.

Bregenz, like Lindau, is situated on the shores of Lake Constance, right up against the mountain. From the Pfander, which can be reached by cable car, it is possible to see the Allgau Alps, and the Swiss Santis and Altmann ranges, while spread out below are the peaceful waters of the lake.

Bregenz is a charming town located at the gateway to the vast Alpine regions which cover 71% of Austrian territory. It is particularly popular with watersports enthusiasts. It also has a famous festival. The lower part of the town contains the charming Vorarlberg Museum. Saint Martin's Tower and the 14th-century church of Saint Gall, with its strange belltower-porch, are the prominent landmarks of the upper part.

Crossing the Vorarlberg there are three routes which lead into the Tyrol, the first of these passing through the Bregenzerwald.

The Bregenzerwald is a wide and twisting valley bordered by rocky barriers eroded by the stormy

waters of the Bregenzer Ache. At the Hochkrumbachsattel (5,495 ft.), the Widderstein (8,320 ft.) towers over the pass. Further north we come to the mountain ranges which enclose the beautiful Klein Walsertal Valley, which can be reached only via Oberstdorf, in Bavaria. The huge slopes of Lech, Oberlech and Zurs, three internationally famous resorts, stretch away to the south. After the Flexenpass (5,853 ft.) the road begins its spectacular descent towards the Arlberg, passing, on the way, through a number of galleries built as protection against avalanches.

The direct route to the Arlberg Pass crosses the middle of the Vorarlberg passing through Feldkirch, a town full of painted houses, above which Schattenburg Castle occupies a dominant position. From the industrial city of Bludenz the road climbs towards the pass in stages, across the Klostertal, the narrow valley at the bottom of which the road winds its way through a number of small villages. The single-track railroad carrying international traffic winds its way, with the help of numerous tunnels and other feats of engineering, across rock faces bristling with avalanche barriers.

Bludenz also opens onto the imposing Brandnertal Valley, and, in the south, on the high Alpine road to the Silvretta. Montafon Valley is pleasang and fertile, and assumes its Alpine appearance as soon as it reaches the delightful resorts of Schruns and Tschagguns. From Partenen the road climbs 3,280 ft. through an impressive series of hairpin bends to reach Vermunt Lake at 5,719 ft., where it ends. The turquoise waters of the man-made Lake Silvretta, at an altitude of 6,660 ft., are situated at the top of the Tyrolean slopes which lead down to Paznauntal.

In the Austrian Alps: left, the peaks of the Vorarlberg and the Heiligengut, on the road to the Grossglockner; right, Bregenz, on Lake Constance, and the fashionable resort of Lech am Arlberg.

for a stopover, with excellent facilities, is situated in a wide sunlit basin. A festival which has its origins in pre-Christian times—the Masquerade of the Phantoms—takes place here once every four years.

Near Innsbruck, on the wide fertile plain where cereals and fruit are grown, stands the impressive outline of the white and ochre Cistercian Abbey of Stams, a masterpiece of Austrian Baroque architecture.

Innsbruck, the Tyrolean capital (1,884 ft.) is one of the few big cities in the heart of the Alps. The beauty and splendor of the city can be seen

INNSBRUCK AND THE INN VALLEY

The Inn enters the Tyrol at the mouth of the Basse-Engadine in Switzerland. Disregarding the fork which leads off to the nearby Southern Tyroal, the Alpine river flows capriciously, to either right or left of the road, reaching Kufstein, 115 miles further on, at the gateway to Bavaria.

After emerging from the wild Finstermunz Gorges, the picturesque high valley of the Inn, hemmed in by wooded mountains, stretches in a straight line from Pfunds-Stuben, with its typical oriel-window houses, as far as Ried. At a bend in the river is Fliess, a summer resort whose houses

are spread out in a verdant setting. Landech, a small industrial town and major communications center, is well known because of its stoutly-built 13th-century fortress.

This and other ruined fortresses such as Schrofenstein, which stands on the opposite side of the valley, and Kronburg, show the strategic importance of this ancient crossroads. From Zams onwards, the Inn Valley loses its verdant appearance. Boxed in between bare limestone slopes and dark fir forests, the valley basin has room only for the river, the road and the single-track railroad. Then the countryside become brighter and the valley more pleasant. Imst, an ideal place

68

from the Hafelekar (6,574 ft.) and the Patscherko-flel (7,372 ft.) which are accessible by cable car. Marie-Theresienstrasse offers one of the best views of the snow-fringed Nordkette, whose steep slopes stretch down almost to the roof tops. In the foreground, the Little Golden Roof—a delightful

Left, the 15th-century House with the Little Gold Roof, at Innsbruck, the capital of the Tyrol; general view of the town; the banks of the Inn and the Maria-Theresienstrasse, in the center of the town.

building for which we are indebted to Maximilian I's taste for ostentation—is framed by two bulbous belltowers. That same prince's sumptuous mausoleum is situated in the Hofkirche, near the Hofburg, the residence of the Hapsburgs. The Silver Chapel towers over the monument, which is surrounded by twenty-eight bronze statues known as the Black Gentlemen.

To get an idea of local traditions, one should really make a trip to the Museum of Tyrolean Folk Art, and attend one of the Tyrolean Evenings which are so popular with tourists all year round.

Since the holding of the Winter Olympics at Innsbruck in 1964, the town has expanded its sporting facilities, and nearby resorts such as Igls also attract many skiers.

In the lower Inn Valley places like Solbad Hall and Schwaz, which were once very prosperous, deserve a stopover, before one moves on to the broad and beautiful basin which leads to Kufstein.

This town, whose most prominent landmarks are a towering rockface and a 13th-century fortress, is visited by large numbers of tourists throughout the year.

THE NORTHERN TYROL, A SKIER'S PARADISE

Foreign tourists often regard Austria as consisting of the Tyrol and little else. The mere mention of the name brings to mind a string of cliches. The neat houses with painted window frames and flower-laden balconies, spread out on an intensely green slope, just below the edge of a dark pine forest; the slender red belltower of the village church rises against a background of snow-capped rocky peaks. A wooden covered bridge crosses the foaming turquoise waters of a mountain stream. A

calvary protected by a roof, both of them the work of a local sculptor, stands at a crossroads surrounded by a wealth of wild flowers. The statue of Saint John Nepomucenus looks down over the fountains in the villages, of which he is the patron saint. On Sunday the villagers leave church attired in their Sunday best: the *dirndl,* a tight-fitting bodice and small crimped apron, for the women, and a hunting suit for the men—grey with green ornaments and horn buttons, plus the ubiquitous Tyrolean hat. The parishioners then go off to the local inn, with its *Blaskapelle,* or local band. Traditional costumes, loden coats, yodelling and beer: a well-deserved rest and relaxation,

as the hay is drying—erected on wooden crosses—on the splendid slopes which, a few months later, will be covered with skiers.

The Tyrol is a paradise for alpine sports: in summer, scaling the lofty peaks where the wonderful upland wild flowers grow and where the nervous marmot hisses; and, in winter, skiing at a large number of comfortable resorts.

St. Anton, which has enjoyed immense prestige since Hannes Schneider developed the Arlberg Method there in 1907, shares with St. Christoph a superbly laid out skiing area. A series of cable cars take one to Vallugagipfel (9,222 ft.), from which there is a remarkable view of the Lechtal Alps, the peaks of the Verwall and the Silvretta. The Arlberg Pass, which was once quite a difficult challenge in winter, is now a most uneventful part of one's journey, thanks to a number of international express trains and a recently-built protected road which then takes one on to other valleys.

Lermoos and Ehrwald, two other famous resorts, are situated in the upper Loisach Valley in the midst of exceptionally beautiful scenery. Cable cars which are among the highest in the Alps take one from Ehrwald to the top of the Zugspitze (9,730 ft.).

The elegant resort of Seefeld, which overlooks the Inn Valley, stands out against the background of the Wetterstein and the Karwendel. The steep-sided Achensee, the biggest lake in the Tyrol and one of the most beautiful in the Alps generally, is situated in this massif.

The imposing Kaisergebirge massif runs along the Bavarian frontier towards Salzburg. St. Johann in Tirol occupies a most exceptional site within the massif, being so close to the Kitzbüheler Horn (6,548 ft.) from which there is a splendid view of the Grossglockner and the Gross Venediger. Kitzbühel, on the other side, is a world famous resort, known particularly for its famous Hahnenkamm descent, on which the most experienced of the world's skiers compete. At the 1956 Winter Olympics, Toni Sailer, who was brought up in the Kitzbühel area, won a brilliant triple victory which is still a source of pride to the townspeople.

The Tyrolean Alps. Above, panoramic view; the famous resort of Kitzbühel and Seefeld. Facing, left and right, landscapes around the Kaisergebirge, in spring and at harvest time. Following pages: winter wonderland at Badgastein, on the northern slopes of the Tauern.

CLIMBING HIGH IN THE SOUTH TYROL

The main valleys which cross the South Tyrol—the upper Inn Valley, the Otztal and the Brenner Pass,—are very popular routes into the South Tyrol. Thanks to the picturesque and winding route via the Fernpass, in the North Tyrol, Bavaria and Italy are thus virtually next door to each other. However, the southern valleys, on account of their mild climate and their proximity to the peaks and glaciers of the Greater Alps, are excellent places to stay.

The slopes of the Paznauntal, along the Silvretta route, constitute the western border of this region, which contains some pleasant ski and vacation resorts, such as Ischgl and Kappl. Trisanna Bridge, next to Wiesberg Castle below the snow-capped ridges of the Parseierspitze (9,967 ft.), stands at the entrance to the valley, nearly three hundred feet above the surging waters of the torrent. The nearby resorts of Serfaus, Ladis and Bad Obladis are frequented by skiers, mountain-climbers and persons seeking the curative effects of the local water.

The wild romantic valleys of the Kaunertal and the Pitztal are among the most beautiful in the Tyrol. The Kaunertal, which is enclosed by the Gepatsch Glacier (9,843 ft.), the biggest in the Austrian Alps, presents experienced climbers with some real challenges. The same is true of the Pitztal, one end of which, at St. Leonhard, is also blocked off by steep mountains.

The Otztal massif is the highest in Austria, with about a hundred peaks of nearly 10,000 ft., and the Wildspitze at 12,382 ft. This is the valley of immaculate glaciers, covering a total surface of 125 square miles, and accordingly is very popular with climbers. The valley, which faces south and is often swept by the *föhn*, begins in a distinctly southern mood at Otz (2,690 ft.) and ends in a wholly mountainous setting at Obergurgl (6,266 ft.), the highest village in the Tyrol and a fine skiing and climbing resort.

The superb Stuibenfall Waterfalls deserve a detour before we return to a number of resorts with an international reputation: Sölden, Hochsölden, Zwieselstein, leading to the Ventertal. A short distance away the Timmelsjoch road climbs through a majestic series of hairpin bends as far as the Italian frontier, at 8,146 ft., in an unforgettable setting of soaring peaks and glistening glaciers.

The Brenner Expressway, which was opened in 1964, is one of the finest and boldest feats of engineering of this century. For twenty-two tortuous miles it winds its way through valleys and across ravines on forty-four bridges, including Europe Bridge, near Innsbruck. This steel and concrete giant, 2,690 ft. long, spans the Sill River at a height of 623 ft. On the way to the Brenner Pass the traveler is treated to some splendid views.

The Zillertal, a valley leading into the lower Inn Valley, contains a number of resorts which are popular with young skiers and climbers. Zell am Ziller and Mayrhofen are renowed for their folk festivals.

Left, the picturesque Austrian Alps: sleighs, as in times gone by, at Serfaus, and a narrow-gauge train at one of the jetties on the Achensee. Above, the Ötztal Massif; below, the Sella Massif seen in the twilight.

A watery paradise: left, the Ferleiten and the Silkmann; above and below, the Krimml Waterfalls; bottom right, Lake Alm, in the Salzkammergut.

THE GIANTS OF THE HOHE TAUERN

The Krimml Falls, west of the Hohe Tauern, between the Kitzbuhel and Zillertal Alps, are among the most impressive in the entire Alpine region. The tumultuous waters of the Krimmler Ache swoop down in cascades into the abyss from a height of over 1,300 feet, in an amphitheater at the end of the Salzach Valley.

The Gross Venediger (12,054 ft.) is situated nearby, separated from the Grossglockner (12,460 ft.), the highest peak in the Austrian Alps, by the Tauerntal. This superb valley, with Matrei in Osttirol, a major touring and mountain-climbing center, attracts numerous visitors. These discover the 'Great Venetian', with its glaciers glistening in the sun, from the magnificent vantage point of Aussergschlöss, at 5,560 ft., on the edge of the Tauerntal in the direction of Lienz.

Lienz, the gateway to Italy and Venice, situated at an altitude of 2,198 ft., is very popular with summer visitors. Its popularity is also due to its remarkable location, at the confluence of the Isel and the Drave, below towering dolomitic ridges and not far from the route around the Gross-glockner, to the south.

This road starts near Zell am See. From the Schmittenhöhe (6,447 ft.), overlooking the pleasant little town on the shores of the lake which bears its name, there is a fine view of the jagged ridges of the Wilder Kaiser, the rocky heaps of the Steinernes Meer and the glaciers of the Hohe Tauern. The nearby valley of Kaprun and its imposing hydroelectric dams can be counted among the giants of the Tauern. Of these, the Grossglockner, at the foot of which they are situated, and its magnificent road, built between 1930 and 1935, are the most representative.

The best time to discoverer the high alpine road to the Grossglockner is early in autumn, when the first frost has cast a reddish tinge over the bare slopes, and when the first snows have clad peaks and glaciers in an immaculate white. This is the season when, moving out of the upland pastures, the flocks descend to the valleys, their heads adorned with ribbons and flowers woven into pyramid patterns, to the tinkling of cowbells. Silence reigns once again in the great natural park of the Hohe Tauern. After Bruck, the road leaves the dark Fusch Valley and climbs to Hochmais (6,070 ft.), opposite the Grossglockner. Then, from the belvedere of the Edelweiss-Strasse, at

8,435 ft., one is treated to a unique panorama including thirty-seven mountains of over 9,000 ft., and nineteen glaciers. Before we come to the Glacier Road, Heiligenblut lies deep inside the beautiful valley, on the way down to Lienz. From the top of the panoramic terrace and from the Franz-Joseph-Haus (7,946 ft.) there is a dazzling view of the Pasterze, the biggest glacier in the eastern Alps (10 miles), stretching out its icy ridges at the foot ot the Grossglockner. Beyond it we come to the domain of the mountain-climber, whose headquarters, at Heiligenblut, is moved here during the summer months.

On the way up from Lienz to Salzburg, via the Tauern Tunnel, we come to two spas situated in picturesque settings well suited for skiing and climbing: Badgastein, noted for its elegance, and Bad Hofgastein, more on the middle class side.

The road to the Grossglockner, the high point of the Austrian Alps, and the chalets of Kals, in the Ködnitz Valley, at the foot of the famous mountain. Facing, Mount Pasterze and the glacier of the same name.

SALZBURG AND THE MIRRORS OF THE SALZKAMMERGUT

The great 19th-century traveler Alexander von Humboldt ranked Salzburg and vicinity as one the "three most beautiful areas in the world". Despite the passage of time the sumptuous city of the Archbishop-Princes has retained much of its former enchantment.

Ringed by bluish muntains which close of the horizon, the wooded slopes of the town's two belvederes—the Kapuzinerberg and the Mönchberg, crowned by the massive Hohensalzburg fortress—rise from the floor of a vast plain. At the foot of the fortress, bounded by the fast-flowing waters of the Salzach, stands the old town, bristling with the belltowers of its magnificent churches, its many squares graced by Baroque fountains and drinking troughs. The narrow Getreidegasse, with its tall houses painted in pastel shades, was where Mozart was born and lived. The lavish residence of the Archbishop-Princes stands next to the beautiful cathedral, built in light marble. The horses of the cabs stir restlessly, their bells tinkling, by the carillon which plays an air from Mozart. The Mirabell Gardens, from which there is a superb view of the town, invite one to rest a while, before going to a concert in the Salzburg Festival or a performance at the Puppet Theater. From the nearby Untersberg, the summit of which can be reached by a cable car which carries one across huge abysses, there is a vast sweeping panorama of the Bavarian Alps and Salzburg.

The Salzkammergut starts after the fine road to the Gaisberg (4,226 ft.), just outside Salzburg. This region, which is divided between three *Länder*—Salzburg, Upper Austria and Styria—owed its wealth in centuries past to the extraction of salt. Nowadays it is a popular tourist area, thanks to a combination of water sports and the pleasures of mountain and skiing.

From the Fuschlsee there is a succession of lakes. First comes the Wolfgangsee,which stretches out below the Schafberg (5,853 ft.), with St. Gilgen and St. Wolfgang, two neat and

attractive resorts. St. Wolfgang, once a place of
pilgrimage, has a church containing a priceless
alterpiece by Michael Pacher. Nearby is the
famous White Horse Inn—which one should not
look for in the Tyrol. A short distance away we
come to the half-moon-shaped Mondsee, the huge
Attersee, which is rather like an inland sea, and
the Traunsee. Gmunden, a most charming resort,
is situated on the shores of the last of these lakes,
the deepest in all of Austria (627 ft.). Bad Ischel,
which was a brilliant gathering-place for high
society and artists in the 19th century, surrounded
by splendid wooded mountains, has lost none of
its appeal. Clinging to a foothill of the Dachstein,
Hallstatt casts reflections of its romantic image in
the dark waters of the lake which bears its name.
The Gosausee lies among some truly majestic
scenery, partly within the imposing Dachstein
massif (9,826 ft.).

From the remarkable vantage point at the top
of the Krippenstein (6,920 ft.), which can be
reached by cable car, there is a superb view of the
Dachstein group of mountains with their huge
caves of ice, on a wild upland plateau dotted with
steep peaks, onto which only seasoned athletes
should venture.

**Right, Hallstatt, on the Lake of the same name, a
place famous for its Celtic metropolis, and a view
of Salzburg, the birthplace of Mozart. Above, a
valley in this region, with a view of the Kleinvene-
diger. Right, Zell am See.**

FROM THE AUSTRIAN RIVIERA TO THE VALLEY OF HELL

Separated from the Salzkammergut by the Niedere Tauern, Carinthia owes the mildness of its climate to that rocky barrier against the north winds. Its bright golden light has a distinctly southern air about it. The warm waters of its lakes —more than two hundred of them!—draw tourists from spring to autumn.

Spittal an der Drau, at the foot of the Goldeck (7,018 ft.) provides us with a foretaste of Italian art with the Château Porcia, and its fine Renaissance courtyard and galleries. Millstatt, one of the most popular resorts in Carinthia, is a short distance away. Its lake, with its giant diving platform, stands out against the background of the snowcapped foothills of the Tauern. Its 11th-century Benedictine abbey is famous for its Romanesque sculptures, which are among the most beautiful in Austria.

There are some fine vantage points, such as the Gerlitzen (6,263 ft.) and the Kanzel (4,921 ft.), which offer excellent views of the lakes of Ossiach and Wörth, both of which lie at the foot of the Karawanken, whose highest point is at 7,030 ft.

The Benedictine abbey of Ossiach, which is located in rather an austere setting, once received a most august visitor: Charles V.

Shortly after the medieval castle of Landskron we come to the Wörthersee. Two towns are situated on the shores of this lake, the biggest in Carinthia: Velden, a lively resort, and Pörtschach. This major boating center, which is famous for its regattas, enjoys a superb position, on a peninsula, with flowers down the water's edge, against the majestic background of the successive ridges of the Karawanken. Klagenfurt, the capital of Carinthia, is nearby, and deserves a visit on account of its interesting regional museum.

After the smiling landscape of Carinthia come the relatively unpopulated valleys of Styria, enclosed within the wooded Pannonic Alps, which end not far from Graz, its capital. The wilder side of Styria appears in the Gesäuse Ravine, a series of steep-walled gorges in the shadow of the Hochtor (7,760 ft.) and opening onto the Eisenerz basin. In a plain covered with black dust stands the rust-colored mountain of iron, the Erzberg (4,921 ft.), whose tiered segments are being worked in an opencast mining operation. From the Polster (6,270 ft.) there is a fine panorama of the Eisnerz Alps, the Ennstal and the Hochswab. The delightful Leopoldsteinersee, enclosed within rock walls some of which drop sheer down into the dark waters of the lake, lies in this massif.

On the way to our trip through the Höllental (Valley of Hell) we pass through Bruck an der Mur, with the beautiful ironwork of its 17th-century fountain, Mariazell, a celebrated shrine and winter sports center, and also Semmering, all of which are excellent stopovers. This remarkable valley, where the Viennese love to go on strips as well as for training, provides us with a final majestic view of the Austrian Alps. With the Kaiserstein (6,762 ft.) and the Klosterwappen (6,808 ft.) towering over it, the valley is hemmed in between the Raxalpe and the Schneeberg, its steep rocky walls lined with pines which cling on against great odds. The green waters of the Schwarza leap tumultuously from one boulder to another at their feet.

In Carinthia. The forest and a detail of a rustic dwelling. Right, a landscape in the southern part of the province.

THE PIEMONT ALPS

Virtually the whole of the southern slopes of the Alpine massif consists of the Italian Alps, forming a natural boundary between Italy and France, Switzerland, Austria and Yugoslavia. Their most notable feature, however, is that they lead us into another world, and another climate.

Though still unmistakably Alpine, these mountains have a breath of the Mediterranean about them: a warmer air, a different light, and, in some places, another kind of vegetation!

This is certainly true even of the Piedmont Alps, which face eastwards; they close the arc of the massif, and, from the Mediterranean to the Lake Léman, fall away steeply to the plains below, along parallel valleys whose waters flow into the Po.

The highest peak of the southern part, Cuneo (Coni), is at an altitude of only 1,640 ft., some fifteen miles as the crow flies from the Argentera (11,800 ft.). Suse, which is closer to Mount Cenis (11,483 ft.), is also only 1,640 ft. above sea level. Aosta, at 1,903 ft., is located at the foot of the prodigious massifs of the Grand Paradis, Mont-Blanc and the Matterhorn.

This towering barrier is crossed by a number of passes, used throughout history by merchants and migrants, as well as by invaders, from Hannibal in 217 B.C. to Napoleon in 1796.

In the southern part of the range the passes have been opened more recently: the Col de Tende, above Limone-Piemonte, a winter sports resort, the Col de la Lombarde, at more than 6,560 ft., and the Col de la Maddalena. Further to the north, the Mount Viso massif stands impregnable, blocking off all access to France.

Sestrières, on the other hand, has the advantage of dual access, by road and rail.

However, the Valle d'Aosta, with its diversity and its climate, is without a doubt the finest part of the Piedmont Alps. This valley, which runs for more than sixty miles, lavishing all the natural charms of the mountains on its visitors, backs up on the Mont Blanc massif, with the Dora Baltea river running through it.

As a result of its Savoyard past, the Valle d'Aosta, which has been a thoroughfare since Roman times, retains many French place-names: Pont-Saint-Martin, Pré Saint-Didier, Chatillon, Saint-Vincent. Protected by the towering mountains which surround it, and exposed to the warm winds from the south, this is a valley where almond and peach trees bloom, and where vineyards and fig-trees grow. It still has its old villages with their stone slab roofs, haylofts, and on their lush slopes, flocks of sheep. The glories of the past are still brought to mind, here and there, by the sight of castles and fortresses.

Winter and summer resorts are situated on the sides of the Grand Paradis, south of the valley, at the food of the Matterhorn in the north, with Valtournanche and Breuil-Cervinia, at 6,726 ft., in an admirable amphitheater of towering peaks.

To the east we come to Courmayeur, the Italian Chamonix, at the mouth of the Mont-Blanc tunnel. One hopes that this new road link will not destroy the charm which the valley has managed to preserve so far, nor that of its capital city, Aosta.

In the Valle d'Aosta. A peak of the Grand Paradis, Pic Castello, the castle of Saint-Nicolas and the setting of Courmayeur. Right, the gorges carved out by the Rocciamelone Torrent, haymaking and a rustic chapel amidst the snow-covered fields. Lake Como (the most varied of all the Italian lakes) seen from Varenna.

THE ITALIAN LAKE DISTRICT

Between the Swiss Alps and the Lombard plain, the lake district is one of the attractions of northern Italy. This Alpine area is bounded by two large massifs: Monte-Rosa (15,203 ft.) in the west, and the Bernina (13,303 ft.) in the east.

A number of larges lakes, formed during the ice ages, are situated between them at the edge of the plain; like Lake Léman they constitute a lakeside Riviera. Its southerly connection brings the region the benefits of mild temperatures.

The area at the foot of Monte Rosa is popular with skiers and climbers. Macugnaga consists of a number of villages which are visited all year round by mountain-lovers.

From there, or from Domodossola, at the foot of the Simplon Pass—a major road link between Italy and Switzerland, we enter the lake district, coming first to Lake Orta, which, though small, is nonetheless one of the more charming ones, in its lush landscape. The Mattarone range lies between it and Lake Maggiore, which stretches all the way from Locarno, in Switzerland, to Arena—a length of some forty miles. The showpiece of the lake is Stresa, an elegant international vacation spot with the palatial hotels and sumptuous gardens of a bygone age.

From a jetty on the fine lakefront promenade, boats go to the charming Borromean Islands, just offshore. There are three islands, each of them tinged with legend: Isola Bella, with its baroque palace, furniture and collections, and its terraced gardens with their lush vegetation. Isola Madre consists of a botanical garden, while Isola dei Pescatori adds the charm of picturesque old houses and narrow streets.

There are other towns along the lake shore: Verbania, Baveno, with its church in the Lombard style, and Arena in the south.

No visitor to the Italian Alps should neglect the lakes which lie at their feet. Quite as much as the glaciers flowing on the high slopes, they are the product of the mountains themselves. On the threshold of the harsh grandeur of the Alps, they represent a mood of gentle living, the *dolce vita* so dear to Italy.

Beyond Lake Maggiore we come to Lake Lugano, of which only one side is Italian, and Lake Como, matched by Lake Lecco at the Bellagio promontory, which is famous for its fine villas and lovely walks. There are a number of towns at the foot of the mountains: Managgio, Tremezza and Lenno—the Riviera Tremezzina, and its princely 18th-century villas, where the Lombard and Austrian aristocracy used to desport themselves. Lastly we come to the lively town of Como, with its terrace cafés, its cathedral and its old walls. In order to get a good view of the entire lake it is necessary to climb up to Brunate.

Further east is the less well known and smaller Lake Iseo, with the solitary Monte Isola standing, belvedere-like, in the midst of its waters. Lake Garda stretches all the way from the mountains to

the plain, between the high peaks of the Altissimo and the Sirmione Peninsula, to the south, a spa protected by Scaligero castle, complete with drawbridge, keep and battlements. Riva, in the north, marks the beginning of the road to the Brenta massif and has a pleasant beach next to a park graced by magnolias. At Gargnano and Limone del Garda, orange and lemon trees grow on terraces along the shores of the lake.

Above, the shores of Lake Garda and the fortress of Sirmione. Right, two views of Lake Como, and one of the famous Borromean Islands, in the heart of Lake Maggiore.

ALTO ADIGE AND THE DOLOMITES

At eastern part of the Italian Alps has two different faces: Trentino—Alto Adige, between the Austrian frontier and Lake Garda, and, further eastwards, the Dolomites, which continue, in the form of the Carnic Alps and the Julian Alps, to the northeast frontier of Italy and to Yugoslavia, respectively.

The Brenner Pass, situated at 4,500 ft. on the Austro-Italian border, is a major crossing between the Germanic and Latin worlds. Drusus, grandson of Augustus, is said to have been the first to have traveled through the pass, in 15 B.C. Later on it became a major Roman highway, along which the barbarian hordes streamed southwards in the 5th century.

Nowadays the pass road divides in two at Vitipeno, one branch going towards Bressanone, and the other towards Merano, via the Passo di Giovo (6,870 ft.), from which there is a commanding view of the Otztal Glacier. The two roads join up again at Bolzano, where the charm of Italy makes its appearance once again, among the domes and campaniles near the palaces of the Austrian princes.

Bolzano, the capital of Alto Adige, has retained its medieval district, and, like Bressanone, a number of distinctly Germanic monuments. Further on, the beautiful valley of the Adige spreads out its pastures and forests at the foot of the Brenta massif.

Trent is on the way to Lake Garda, Verona and Venice. It is a good touring base and a historic city, which was often the subject of contention between Austria, Bavaria and Italy.

Majestic and rugged scenery in the Dolomites. Above: the Cime di Lavaredo (9,835 ft.); below, lakes Fregabolgia and Rotondo; right, the "pyramids" of Segonzano, in the Val di Fiemme.

East of the main Brenner road at Trent we come to the Dolomites, whose highest peak, the Marmolada, rises to 10,965 ft. The most remarkable thing about the Dolomites, however, is their geology and their striking appearance. Depending on the light at any particular time of day, the jagged ridges of pink limestone, which stretch like huge cliffs for many hundreds of feet, take on a range of colors which are sheer magic. The three peaks of the Lavaredo rear their gigantic spurs to altitudes of nearly 10,000 ft.

Besides being a paradise for mountain climbers and hikers, the Dolomites also provides skiers with a choice of resorts, from Brunico to Belluno.

Top prize in this respect definitely goes to Cortina d'Ampezzo (4,016 ft.)—a resort with excellent facilities and accomodation, in a magnificent setting, ringed by southward-facing mountains. The ski-runs, ski-lifts, cable cars and modern stadium are all due to the holding of the Winter Olympics at Cortina in 1956.

The Dolomites. The Torre Toblino and the Cima dei tre Scarperi. Below, the ascent of the Sautner. Right, Cortina d'Ampezzo and the surrounding landscape.

THE SLOVENE ALPS

Slovenia, on of the Yugoslav republics, is even more reminiscent of the typical landscapes of Austria than is the Alto Adige. The Julian Alps, east of the capital, mark the frontier with Italy, while the alpine massif continues northwards along the Austrian frontier as far as Maribor, through which the Drava flows, having made its entry into Yugoslavia at the foot of the Pohorje massif.

The imposing Mount Triglav (9,393 ft.) owes its name, which means 'three-headed', to a legend in which a chamois with golden horns had to guard a treasure which hunters were trying to take from him. This is an exciting area of dolomitic spurs, waterfalls and mountain springs, above valleys with picturesque old villages and meadows surrounded by forests.

There are a number of shelters on the way up Mount Triglav: Triglawski-Dom, or Planika, at 7,900 ft., and Staniceva Koca (7,618 ft.) overlooking the Triglav Glacier.

At the foot of the range which runs along the Italian frontier a fine mountain road leads from Nova Gorica to Kranjka Gora, near the Austrian border.

The Talminka and Kolovrat gorges, at the midway point, are in good skiing country. The best-equipped resorts of the region include Rotece-Planika, a center for competitive skiing, Polkoren, at the foot of Koren Pass, which leads into Austria. Kranj, in the valley of the Save, and Godz Martuljek are good starting points for trips into the massif of the same name, towards Mount Spik (8,110 ft.), the high point of what are commonly called the Slovenian Dolomites.

East of the region, the village of Jesersko leads to Mount Grintavec (8,392 ft.), in the Kamnik Alps. This part of Slovenia, the most southerly

bastion of the alpine massif, is clearly a great touristic asset.

The area is dotted with old churches, as well as monasteries adorned with frescoes (Zirovnica), while the more romantically inclined may prefer the delightful and superbly equipped resort of Bled, at 1,640 ft. A lake carved out by glaciers stretches out at the foot of the resort, in the midst of wooded hills. An 11th-century castle stands on a sheer cliff at the lakeside. It contains a chapel, an archeological museum and some frescoes. From a terrace at the water's edge there is a marvelous view of the Julian Alps. The church of Saint Mary of the Lake, in the Baroque style, is situated on a small island in the middle of the lake.

In Slovenia: the Kamnik Alps. To and facing: the romantic setting of Bled, on the shores of a lake of glaciary origin. Right, Podkoren, in the Julian Alps.

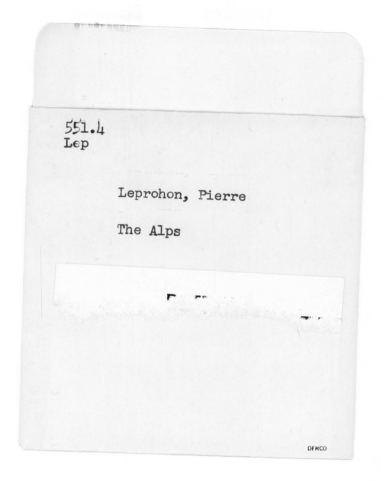